Praise for Kathy

"Photos, memories, and family stories told around the kitchen table are all a part of the tapestry of our lives and Mrs. Widener has done an amazing job of weaving these all together to tell her family's story. Her first two books "Where Memories Live" and "The Return Home" allow us to visit Rayflin, a small back-country South Carolina community long forgotten by most but brought vividly to life to the reader through her wonderful storytelling. The diversity of the characters you'll meet are made flesh and blood and the joys and sorrows of their lives are deeply conveyed. Opening Mrs. Widener's books are like discovering a long lost trunk in the attic filled with wonderful mementos of the past. When the trilogy is completed, Rayflin and its delightful inhabitants will live on once more."

— *George Wingard,* Program Coordinator, Savannah River Archaeological Research Program; Director of "Mart to Art: A Repurposed Life", "The Burnt Church: An Exploration of Pon Pon Chapel of Ease" and "One More Time: Walking the Streets of Dunbarton"

"Kathy Widener writes with an authentic Southern voice. Readers from the South will find plenty to relate to, and those not from here will get a true-to-life glimpse into our culture."

—*Bryce Gibson,* author of *Southern Teen Thrillers*

Also by Kathy Widener

RAYFLIN: WHERE MEMORIES LIVE
RAYFLIN: THE RETURN HOME

the southern child

the southern child

Kathy G. Widener

Deeds Publishing | Atlanta

Copyright © 2019—Kathy G. Widener

ALL RIGHTS RESERVED—No part of this book may be reproduced in any form or by any electronic or mechanical means, including information storage and retrieval systems, without permission in writing from the authors, except by a reviewer who may quote brief passages in a review.

Published by Deeds Publishing in Athens, GA
www.deedspublishing.com

Printed in The United States of America

Cover design by Mark Babcock
Text layout by Matt King

Library of Congress Cataloging-in-Publications data is available upon request.

ISBN 978-1-947309-85-2

Books are available in quantity for promotional or premium use. For information, email info@deedspublishing.com.

First Edition, 2019

10 9 8 7 6 5 4 3 2 1

For

My Siblings
Louise, Lula Mae
and Steve

And to honor
The Memory of Grandma Florence
1887-1974

Contents

Praise for Kathy	i
Why…	xi
1. Legacy	1
2. Little Brother, Uncle Leon and Me	6
3. Small Children Find Trouble	12
4. A House Built to Last	17
5. Uncle Leon Takes a Wife	23
6. Excited About School	27
7. Our Momma Was Beautiful	31
8. Abandoned	37
9. Things Change in the Old House	41
10. Christmas Memories	45
11. Thick as Thieves	50
12. Respect for our Elders, Television & Vices	55
13. Weekend Traditions — Building & Church	61
14. Southern Fried	65
15. Grandma, Wisdom and Patience	70
16 Remembering Rayflin	76
17. A Tribute to Our Daddy	81
18. Take your Medicine	84
19. Health and Hygiene	88
20. Changing Seasons	90

21. Special People I Loved	103
22. Aunt Fannie and the Cats	107
23. Our Climbing Tree	112
24. The Local Country Store	116
25. Third Grade Was the Best	121
16. Vacation Bible School	129
27. Rainy Day Fun	136
28. Grandma's Daily Chores	141
29. Planting the Fields	144
30. A Historical Mansion	147
31. A Night-Frightful and Freezing	154
32. Timeless Memories	157
33. What is Death	162
34. Traveling Man	166
35. School & Bus Shenanigans	174
36. Moving Day	181
37. My Daddy Fell in Love	184
38. Lessons Learnedfrom the Old House	186
Epilogue	189
The Southern Child Lives On	192
Photographs	198

Why...

Why did I decide to write this memoir, Southern Child? My life was not extraordinary. I never traveled the world, associated with famous people, or invented anything considered important to mankind. I lived a pretty ordinary life for the time period and the place I grew up, but maybe that is what makes my story interesting. I grew up in the 1950's in the deep South on a lonely dirt road. My siblings and I lived lives filled with freedom to roam the woods, and stayed outdoors until the sun began to set over the river swamp. We spent our days exploring the woods and fields with our three dogs; searching for blackberries, gooseberries, and plums in the summer. When not in school we were outdoors, dreaming up something to entertain us. We only got toys at Christmas, not enough to last the whole year. The few toys we had, we treasured, and kept them for inside play. We did have a few chores, carrying in buckets of water and filling the wood boxes on the porch in the winter. Otherwise, we were too busy exercising our imaginations in ways country children of limited financial means had to do. The first almost-twelve years of my life, I spent in the same old unpainted clapboard house my Granddaddy Kelly and his brothers built in 1912. That's what

I decided my memoir would be about, growing up in that old house.

I started with a blank journal my sister gave me and began writing down every memory I recalled from my childhood. There was no order to my memories, large or small. They came so fast, one sparking the next. It was as if I lit a string of firecrackers and each exploded, igniting another. I wrote for hours until my thumb and fingers on my right hand were numb, an indentation from the pen painful between the index and middle finger. Every smell, taste, sight, sound, and touch covered pages. It was surprising how much and how long ago I could remember. I'm guessing that is a genetic thing, my long memory. I finally had to take a break because of my sore fingers.

When I began anew, it was miraculous that I could remember in detail what the inside of that old house looked like when I lived there. The patterns and colors of the linoleum and rugs on the floors, subjects and colors of pictures on the walls, and the placement of furniture in the rooms are all images I could visualize. My mind was flooded with memories and my fingers flew over the pages, like a flock of blackbirds on the wing. I wrote so fast when I finally exhausted what I recalled about those years, I could hardly read the words, my writing was so sloppy.

My favorite smells came from my Grandma's rosebush under the kitchen window, honeysuckle blooming beside the road, and the smell of a summer rain soaking into the dry cornfield behind the car-shed. The sound of a rain coming across that same field was a favorite sound along with rain falling on our tin roof to lull me to sleep and the music my daddy played, his voice singing in rhythm with his guitar. Seeing the orange and pink sunsets over the tall junipers below the spring and flocks of birds flying in unison then abruptly changing direction are sights that are seared in my memory for my lifetime. I'll also never forget the feel of wiggling my toes in the damp sand beside the road after a rain, and the warmth of a washtub full of water that has been left in the sunshine to heat for a long-needed bath. It felt so good to be clean from that tub or from playing in the pond up the road, I'd stay until my fingers were wrinkled from so long in the water. The taste of my Grandma's cooking remains with me, too. She was a wonderful cook and would have some treat ready when we got home from school. I only regret I never asked how she made a coffee-flavored icing for her cake. She never used a recipe or measured ingredients.

I know some of my memories may be different from my siblings, but the memories recorded in this memoir are mine alone. I hope those who read these pages agree that nothing is more important than our memories. Mark Twain said, "The two most important days in your life are the day you were born and the day you find out why." It occurs to me that recording my memories and those of my family may just be my why.

1. Legacy

The old house Kelly Gantt and his brothers built in 1912 still stands on the incline above the spring and swamp. I was born ten months after Kelly passed away. He was my grandfather, a real man of distinct character. Stories of him revealed facets of humor, kindness, and if threatened, danger. He did not go looking for a fight but always carried a sharp knife and, more often than not, a loaded pistol.

As long as people lived that had known him, stories would circulate about his exploits and entertain all who witnessed these stories. I never had the privilege of knowing him personally, but the connection is there. I was told so many things about him growing up, all the stories of him and his brothers running moonshine stills in the swamp, resorting to violence when deemed necessary, and having clandestine meetings with women. Even what foods he refused to eat. He didn't care for oysters, didn't eat lettuce, and never would touch a mushroom; he said he wouldn't eat anything that grew in cow shit.

There are lots of old pictures; the confident young man in the derby hat, the middle-age man standing in the walkway in front of his house holding his shotgun, and the crippled old man with a scowl on his face propped up between Robert and Florence. He was quite the character. For better or worse, Kelly Gantt left his mark on this world.

My two sisters, my brother, and I grew up in that old house. Our lives were synonymous to my grandfather's minus the pistols, running from the law, and the moonshine production and consumption.

Granddaddy Kelly by all accounts was well-liked by his friends and respected by his enemies. In his younger years he had a few run-ins with men. More times than not he was taking up for others who were treated shabbily because they were old, weak, kids, or just a different color. His main nemesis was his brother-in-law, Olin Rish. Kelly tolerated him, mostly because he loved his sister Jennie, figuring Olin controlled her and engineered the takeover of the whole of the Gantt property.

Kelly was completely incapacitated in January 1940 by a stroke that destroyed all feeling to his left side, rendering it almost completely useless. He lived with that handicap for the last eleven years of his life. All pictures I have of him after the stroke show a bitter old man. None show him happy or smiling. He was mostly confined to what was then the front parlor. It became his and Grandma Florence's bedroom. He had his radio and his pipe for company. Occasionally he had visitors. His brothers would come, bring a bottle and Florence had no objection to them pouring Kelly a small glass of moonshine. They didn't produce their own any more of course, they were getting too old. During the war years, Robert and his band had square dances, several times in the old house. That's when Kelly seemed to be the happiest.

The younger men would gravitate to Kelly's room just to hear his stories and he had some good ones. He would hold court with three or four of the dance attendees who came more for the fellowship than the dancing. Someone always brought a jug and they knew Mr. Kelly was a magnificent storyteller. They would drag in a couple of extra chairs, share a drink, and Kelly would spin a tale about drinking and what quandaries he got himself into, with a little help from his brothers and some of his drinking friends.

Kelly did love to smoke his pipe and had mastered opening the bag of fragrant tobacco. He would pull the string tie open with his teeth, close it tight with his right hand, and pack the bowl of his pipe with the tobacco. Then he would strike the large wooden matches on the wall beside the fireplace. Over the years there was a definite mark on the wall, the wood was much lighter from the frequent striking of his matches.

Lighting his pipe was always the first thing before beginning a storytelling session with his rapt audience. Those guests suggested they would be glad to help, but he insisted he appreciated their offer but was quite capable.

His eyes would twinkle, and then he would begin his story. Telling about the time him and his buddies, all drunk of course, rode on the back of a flatbed truck. The dirt road was full of potholes brimming with muddy water. Kelly was hanging on to one of the standards on the back when the back wheel abruptly hit a huge mud hole. The standard came out along with Kelly; he landed head first in a water hole. One of the other drunks had sense enough to pound on the driver's door.

"Toby, you have to stop the truck, we've lost Mr. Kelly."

Of course Kelly was so drunk, he didn't remember a thing.

The others collected him and continued on their way. When his younger audience heard that story they would break out in guffaws, pat each other on the back, and insist he tell another. As for his reaction, his old eyes would crinkle and his face, deeply creased from his grouchy demeanor, would immediately break out in a huge smile. He loved to entertain and this was just one of many stories he repeated while he puffed his pipe and sipped his moonshine. It made him feel useful for others to seek his company. For just a little while he could forget his handicap and enjoy being the center of attention.

He was, of course, pleased when his grandchildren, Mary Louise born in 1947 and Lula Mae in 1949, were born in the same old house. Louise says she can remember eating off Granddaddy's plate right along with him and how pleased he was to have her company. When he died she said she remembered our cousin, Tony, picking her up so that she could see Granddaddy in his coffin. She was barely over three years old, but I believe it's possible for a child to have vague glimpses from the past when something so traumatic happens.

Finally in 1948 electricity was installed in the old house, so at least I missed the kerosene lamps and candles. That was the biggest change. Everything else about life in the old house I experienced just like my grandparents.

That old house is our legacy. It's still there, thoroughly remodeled by my brother and his family. It's at least one hundred and five years old and looks great. It was built to last. I love to visit. Sometimes I close my eyes and picture what it looked like when we were kids. I still consider it home. It belongs to Kelly Gantt's descendants and is cherished by all of us kids. We have a lot of wonderful memories in that house. As long as they are recorded, maybe our children and grandchildren will read about that time and realize wealth doesn't equal happiness, it's family and memories.

2. Little Brother, Uncle Leon and Me

Memories are like dreams or glimpses into the past. Sometimes I swear I remember something happening, but find out later it was suggestion, a recollection that someone had planted in my memory bank. In other words, I am just channeling a story someone has said about me.

By the time we came to live in the old house with Grandma Florence, my Daddy, Robert, and our Momma, Uncle Leon had mended his ways. He no longer drank liquor, having quit "cold turkey" on July 31, 1937. I'm certain that is the correct date; his memory was like an elephant; he never forgot. He had a lot of his father in him. He could be downright contrary saying exactly what he thought about others and their actions. Uncle Leon wouldn't take any foul-mouthed remarks from a rude person. He could dish it out if necessary in language the target of his wrath would understand. His personality was like his father, Kelly.

Uncle Leon was surprisingly a gentle man when it came to us kids. He gave us all nicknames at birth. Louise was "Tob." When Lula Mae was born he carried Tob in to see the new baby and asked, "Tob, do you see 'Snooche' lying on that bed?" Louise and Lula Mae were both born at home, delivered by Miss Willow Gunter.

He called me "Skeeter" from the day we met. Steve, he called "Buster." Steve and I were born in Batesburg at a small hospital clinic. As we grew older the nicknames disappeared.

It was Louise, Lu and Steve. But all his life he called me Skeeter and nothing else. That's one reason I believe I was his favorite. Of course, he never purposely showed favoritism, just like Daddy didn't. They were both strong role models for my siblings and me. They never showed affection to us with words or hugs and kisses, but we knew they loved us. They were true brothers even though they had different mothers, a fact that never entered the equation.

The old house was, after all, Uncle Leon's, so we lived with him and paid no rent. He had gotten the house when Aunt Jennie gave him the thirty acres of land he requested per their deal. Leon paid the five per cent down on the back taxes in 1949, allowing Aunt Jennie to claim possession of the whole of Kel and Peninnah's property.

When our Granddaddy died, my daddy had already been married to my momma, Sallie Hartley, for four years. Momma was only sixteen when my oldest sibling, Louise, was born. Lula Mae was next; I came along in 1951. Daddy really wanted a son to carry on the family name; instead he had three girls. Finally the only son, Steve, was born in 1953.

The one fortunate asset I possessed besides eventually being keeper of the family history: I was the only child with Daddy's blue eyes. Every gift I received, if it came in different colors, I got it in blue. I had a blue hula hoop, blue bicycle, blue plaid blanket, and blue car coat, etcetera. Don't ask why my coat was called a car coat. It did have a fleece lined zippered hood that when unzipped lay flat on my back. Must have been a '50s thing.

Daddy leaned more toward my brother, because every man wants a son to follow in his footsteps, to carry on the family name. I stood out because I had blue eyes like Daddy. Thinking back now, it is ironic, my brother, Steve, has three blue-eyed sons and five granddaughters. Precious and beautiful granddaughters but not one grandson to carry on the Gantt name. However, Steve has more the temperament of our grandfather, Kelly Gantt. Steve never tries to preserve someone's feelings. Right or wrong, he doesn't mind saying what he thinks. He's always been good at carpentry like all the Gantts and can build most anything. He loves old farm equipment, and has a working sawmill and grist mill.

He and I were especially close as small children. Being the two youngest we played together and got along fine while Louise and Lula Mae were at school.

My earliest memory of living in the old house is a vague memory from about the age of three, if six decades later a person can remember a story from three years old.

Steve was still sleeping in the crib; it was a perfect fit in a niche to the right of the fireplace in our parents' room. I still sucked a bottle and we were handed a full bottle at the same time. I would slurp mine down in record time, then take baby Steve's bottle and give him my empty one. The door that opened into the bedroom was the perfect hideaway behind which I could empty Steve's bottle too. Evidently, I was caught in the act and was watched closely from then on. No more extra bottle for me. I was reminded of this story many times growing up. Maybe I just heard it so much; I just think it is a memory. Uncle Leon was fond of telling this story and laughed with amusement every time. He also loved to tell about the time I pushed baby brother 'Buster' off the high end of our porch.

'Buster' came inside crying, saying, "Kaki pushed me off the porch." I'm sure there were big crocodile tears streaming down his dirty little face. To make the story more convincing, he blubbered between whines, that while he was hanging on with both hands, feet dangling, I pried his little fingers loose, one at the time. This I don't remember, not that I would have any defense for myself. If it really happened, I may have been four and he probably did something to provoke me. Uncle Leon found this also amusing and told and retold the story even after we four children reached adulthood.

I definitely do remember when Uncle Leon, the same person who poured salt in a keg of homebrew at Uncle Buck's, convinced Steve and me that if we wanted to catch a bird, we only needed to pour salt on its tail. We two spent the better part of a whole day trying to sneak up on a bird with the cardboard salt box. All we had to show for our diligence were little piles of salt all over the yard. Uncle Leon got a big kick out of this misadventure too and loved to repeat it. Grandma was not too pleased after we wasted the salt, but we were not punished. Uncle Leon did after all put us up to it.

Before Steve and I actually started to school, Uncle Leon, already in his mid-forties, was our cohort and playmate. I remember once Steve and I changed clothes. He put on my pink dress with hot pink polka dots, and I put on his dungarees and plaid button-up shirt. We wanted to see if Grandma could tell us apart. We must have thought she was stupid. She said nothing about our clothes, not even to inquire about why we did it. She just ignored us. Since it did not have the desired effect of confusing poor old Grandma, we just changed back. That could have come, not from our own little minds, it was quite possible Uncle Leon suggested the idea. I remember doing it, but he may have planted the seed.

He did love to be with us kids. For some reason, he was home during the daytime, maybe working in his fields, I don't remember why. I do remember how exciting it was when we saw that big yellow bus in the afternoons bringing Louise and Lula Mae home from school. Some afternoons or on weekends, Uncle Leon, Steve, and I would play hide-and-seek with our older siblings. The three of us would search for those two, Louise and Lula Mae. They could hide in the "darndest" places: under the house, inside the dark smokehouse, up in one of the Chinaberry trees. Wherever they hid, Uncle Leon could find them, and then the chase was on. When we caught those two, Uncle Leon would tickle them until they squealed with laughter.

I remember once, we kids would stand at the end of our porch beside the road, count to three and run to the high end and jump off as far as we could. We would then make a slash with our foot in the dirt where we landed. The object was, of course, to see who could jump the farthest. We even talked Uncle Leon into participating. Never again would he accept our challenge. Landing in a squat on one leg, he decided he was too old for this game.

He always said there were three things he never had any use

for: a bicycle, a slingshot, and a hammock. He said if he was in a house with one window open, he couldn't hit one of the walls with a slingshot. In other words, the object would fly out that one window.

Besides taking time with us kids, he was a good example. He was always recording things, carrying a little note pad and pen in his pocket. When he thought something was important enough, he would write it in the notepad.

We sure did love Uncle Leon. He would sometimes cuss when he was angry but only damn, s.o.b., bastard, or maybe shit. He never took God's name in vain or used the "f" word. I don't even remember hearing that word until I was in high school. Things were so different when I grew up in the '50s' in the old house.

3. Small Children Find Trouble

One of my earliest memories is of the fenced area in our backyard. Chicken wire surrounded the huge pecan and magnolia trees, a large area maybe fifty-by-fifty feet with a gate facing the center of the backyard, near the house. The whole idea behind the play yard was to keep us safe when we were very young, mainly from wandering off down to the swamp. As soon as we reached four or five years old, the fence was removed. We still pretty much stayed in the backyard. If we went into the woods, we had our dogs to protect us: Susie, Jack, and Sparky. We couldn't leave the yard without them tagging along.

The play-yard, of course, offered its own set of objects that encouraged us to find trouble. The pecan tree dropped pecans on the ground and of course the magnolia dropped its shiny green leaves, brown flower petals and, most dangerous, the cones at the center of the flowers. I'm not familiar with the yearly cycle of the magnolia, but I know it is an evergreen. Still, there were leaves that fell. The leaves were bright green, the back a fuzzy brown. They would cover the ground and get stiff and brittle, crackle under our feet when we played among them, and had to be raked up. The cones burst open and fell to the ground spilling their slender, long red seeds.

Why Lula Mae aka Snooche decided to cram one of the seeds up each of her nostrils, who knows? Her nose immediately started to burn and her breathing, I'm sure, was hampered. Yelling and trying to breathe through her mouth at the same time, she rushed inside to get help. Momma Sallie took a bobby pin and fished the long red seeds out of her nose. Lesson learned: no more magnolia seeds stuck in our nose, ears or, heaven forbid, mouth to ingest.

I was the one that usually found not just trouble, but also pain. One Christmas while Grandma and Momma were mixing up a fruitcake in a big dishpan in our kitchen, we had a visitor. Our pastor from Steadman Church stopped by along with his son. The sofa was in the hallway, probably because the Christmas tree was already in the front window of the living room.

The pastor's son was about my age and we went out on the porch to play. There was a tin insert that covered the fireplace in the living room during warm weather. Since it was Christmastime, the weather was cold. Daddy kept a fire in the fireplace, so the insert had been removed.

The little boy and I were playing on our porch. I was probably three and remember this well. Steve was not playing with us. Too young, I think. We were jumping off the porch beside the steps onto the tin insert. I'm sure it was not intentionally left beside the steps. Probably, it had been shoved up under the house and we pulled it out. But it made a wonderful reverberating noise, almost like distant thunder, when we landed on it. We thought it was great fun and we kept climbing back up the steps to jump again. We did this several times. Then, I slipped and my leg below the knee came down on the upturned edge of the tin insert, and cut my skinny little leg very deep. I wailed in pain and the pastor and Momma came running, picked me up and placed me on the sofa. There wasn't a lot of blood, but I can remember how white the skin in the cut appeared. Later I was taken to the doctor in Wagener, but did not even get stitches, just a tetanus shot and a bandage. My one-inch scar is proof of the incident.

It's hard to believe, we never had any broken bones or serious injuries, though we roamed the woods and the swamp even in the summertime with the dogs. We must have had a guardian angel that watched over us. I don't remember seeing a snake or dangerous animal in our sojourns while staying in that old house. There were bobcats, foxes, possums, and raccoons, possibly wild dogs or hogs. They probably heard us coming and disappeared, not wanting to tangle with four rambunctious kids and three barking dogs.

Once in the summertime, Grandma let us go for a picnic. There was a stream and swampy area that drained into the black waters of the North Edisto River. It was called Coon Branch and was fed by an artesian spring that boiled up constantly at its head through pure white sand.

Our picnic destination was across the big cornfield to the left of the house. We took cheese sandwiches and a couple jars full of sweet tea, sat beside the stream among the trees, undergrowth, and vines. We never thought about how dangerous it could be; there had to be venomous snakes, like rattlesnakes and water moccasins, insects and spiders galore in the thick woods and undergrowth a short distance from our spot. Grandma didn't seem concerned either. We were always going in the swamp and woods behind and across the road from our house, roaming far and wide.

A lot of times we even crawled under our house. It was dark and the dirt was dry and black, almost like smut. When we crawled out, we were filthy. Baths were optional in our childhood. We usually washed off at the outside spigot. I remember it was so hot we would be sweaty and wore a black necklace of dirt collected in the creases under our neck. Sometimes, we could con or beg Daddy into taking us to the pond about two miles up the road. If we went to the pond, Daddy always took a bar of soap and a washcloth to bathe himself. We kids just played in the water and considered ourselves clean when we came out with our finger tips all wrinkled. To us that was a good sign we must be clean.

Thinking back about living in the old house so near the swamp, we had no concern about danger. We did know better than to play in the road, but seriously, I doubt more than half a dozen vehicles passed by our house in a day. It was a sandy, dirt road in the backwoods. If we heard a vehicle coming, chances were good they were coming to our house anyway.

Another interesting thing about the animals in the nearby woods and fields, we never once saw a deer, wild turkey, coyote, or armadillo. Those animals just migrated to the area in the last fifty years. Now the lands where we played are pretty much overrun with them.

Thinking about the woods so full of unseen creatures, I remember the time Steve followed Uncle Leon on a hunting trip with nothing on but a long-sleeved shirt, nothing on the bottom. He was probably still wearing a diaper which evidently fell off. When Uncle Leon realized Buster was following, he picked him up and they went in the woods, probably hunting squirrel. When they returned, it was obvious that Buster had sat on pine straw, because his little behind and private parts were eaten up with redbugs. I think other parts of the country call them chiggers.

My momma used the best treatment she could, covering each bite with a dab of nail polish. I think maybe it smothered the tiny red devils. They were not easy to see, but you could detect them. I have seen them crawling on my legs and they look like very little red spiders. We learned at an early age, sitting on the woodland floor covered in pine straw was not a good idea in the summertime.

4. A House Built to Last

I can close my eyes and transform my memories of the old house into something tangible, something I can touch. I visit there often in my mind, standing in the front yard and traveling back to a different time, the time when I lived in the old house.

The piece of iron rail is still there near the road. It was a piece of rail from the Swamp Rabbit rail-line torn up in 1933. It sticks out above ground maybe four feet and was initially put there by my Granddaddy to keep people from running over some flowering bush planted long ago. It could have also been used as a post on which to tie up horses or buggies. It has been there many years.

The L-shaped porch is the same, although it has been extended around the corner of the kitchen where Grandma's big rosebush used to flourish. When in bloom sweet smells were sent to folks sitting on the front porch in the spring and summer. The kitchen door is also around the corner from the original, but the kitchen is still in the same place, only modern with an added pantry.

The inside of the house was built of what was referred to as bead board and the one-by-six-boards fit together with tongue and groove. Tongue and groove refers to one board fitting into a groove in the top of the previous one. None of the walls were painted; it was all-natural pine wood. The outside was plain pine clapboard, drab and grey from weathering with slashes of orange where "fat lightered" shown through. The high peaked roof of the house, the newer part, and the two-room original were covered with silver painted corrugated tin.

The old kitchen, I remember had a table my granddaddy built covered with an oil cloth. There were no cabinets on the walls then, a stand-alone Hoosier cabinet stood behind the door for dishes. Pots and pans resided in the drawer underneath the cook stove. This old kitchen had a wash stand with a water spigot, a shallow pan to wash hands, an aluminum dipper hanging on a nail to quench thirst, and a medicine cabinet on the wall above. There was a mirror on the door of the cabinet; inside were a straight razor, shaving soap, and a brush to lather menfolk's faces. This medicine cabinet was built by Granddaddy Kelly, along with the washstand, which had a shelf underneath, a curtain tacked all the way around, and red cloth with a pattern of some sort. I don't remember what was stored on the shelf underneath. I do remember the washstand and cabinet were painted an indefinable yellow one could hardly visualize. Even at my tender age, I wondered why they decided on that bright yellow paint. The paint must have been a gift; I can't imagine anyone choosing that color on purpose. It actually made school buses dull in comparison.

The spigot in the old kitchen was the only plumbing inside. Uncle Leon had a pump put down in 1950 and there was a short table built around an outside spigot near one of the huge chinaberry trees in the back yard. There were no indoor bathrooms with tubs or toilets.

The room next door to the kitchen was originally the dining room, but I remember it as Uncle Leon's bedroom; there was a connected entryway from the original two-room house which was opened to the newer part. The door opening was added between the two after Granddaddy Kelly had his stroke in January, 1940. The room beyond that entryway belonged to my two sisters and Grandma Florence. Two iron double beds with cotton tufted and striped mattresses along with Grandma's dresser pretty much filled the room. I slept in the bed with Grandma eventually. There was also an old cabinet that had belonged to Granddaddy Kelly's first wife, Mary. It had no doors, but curtains on the outside were attached by a cord to cover the shelves. It was used to stack our clothes and there was a triangle shaped medal rod which fit over the back of the bedroom door, like a attachment to hang a wreath. This rod is where our dresses hung on wire hangars.

I can't remember my first bed; presumably it was in Momma and Daddy's bedroom. I do remember the crib to the right of the fireplace. Their bedroom was the room at the far end of the large central hall on the right, near the north porch. I can remember when my baby brother, Steve, slept in that crib, so I suppose I did too.

Stepping from the bedroom the girls and Grandma Florence occupied, we entered the wide hallway with doors on both ends. One opened on to the front L-shaped porch, the other onto the north porch. Directly across was the living room, once Granddaddy Kelly and Grandma Florence's room. The hall was wide, six or eight feet, enough space to contain Grandma's trunk, the pie safe, a quilt box, and her peddle sewing machine, all without hindering our walking to and fro.

All the floors were covered in vinyl linoleum 'rugs', no bare wooden boards except around small outer areas where the rugs didn't reach.

The doors on each end of the wide hall had a vertical row of glass on each side of the door. I don't remember any sort of curtain covering what we called the window lights. As a child I was somewhat leery of these windows at night because of the darkness outside. The same was true of the window in our bedroom, only panes of glass and a ruffle for a curtain on top. I imagined someone or something watching us through the black rectangle of darkness, nothing between us and the outside except the glass and a screen. I was thankful, when I slept with Grandma, that my side was by the wall and not the window. I would have glanced up and saw the blackness, probably hiding my head under the covers to remove the temptation to do so. Sometimes I woke up in the middle of the night, so very thirsty. Afraid to stray from the safety of the bed, I would wake Grandma and she would get me a glass of water. More times than not, she didn't even grumble about my waking her up, she was used to the darkness and understood I was just a scared little kid.

In that time period there were scores of country folks that didn't even lock their doors at night, but we always did. It made me feel safer looking at the blackness outside. The only light on the outside of the house was from the moon and the stars, no security lights. There was an electric light on each of the porches, but they were seldom on unless we had visitors after dark.

All the rooms had an electric, insulated cord hanging down in the center with a screw in connector and a light bulb. There were no switches beside the door. When you entered a room, you had to walk blindly to the center and reach upward for the cord with the light bulb and a small chain to pull turning on the light. There was a string cord attached to most of the lights which was easier to locate in the darkness. Just wave your hands until you encounter the cord and pull it. My daddy attached a long string to the chain in his bedroom and attached the other end to the headboard of the bed, making it easy to turn on the light, if need be, in the middle of the night. He could just yank the sting tied to the bed.

Standing at the road, the room at the far right at the back of the house was also a bedroom. My sister remembers that being Uncle Leon's and it may have been. Everyone has different memories, these are mine.

The north porch faced two fields separated by a terrace. This porch was not used to sit in the spring and summer for visiting. It was completely devoid of chairs. There was a board shelf between the column nearest the road and the house, built to hold some of Grandma Florence's potted plants. At one time two clotheslines made of heavy stretched rope crisscrossed the other end. Only small things were hung here, like dirty dishcloths that were washed in a small tub, needing to dry, or maybe rags used to clean spills. Normally no garments hung here unless needed before the next washday.

The main object of this porch was a place for us to play when it poured rain. It stretched across the entire house and had a wide set of steps probably six or eight feet across and a like number of steps to reach the ground. What I remember most about this porch was the fact we played there when the rain poured, pushing each other up and down the length in Steve's peddle-operated red fire engine. I also remember sitting on the steps watching the night sky filled with stars, searching for Russia's Sputnik, the first man-made satellite sent into orbit. That was in 1957 and we thought it was amazing, a little speck of light, just like another star in the heavens, but moving east to west.

The old house was built better than homes of today. We never had a leaky roof when the rains came down. The boards on the porches were regularly replaced if they started to rot under the eaves from the weather, as were the carved posts supporting the roof. There were no sagging floors in any of the rooms and they all were level. Outside steps were regularly replaced if they began to rot at all. It was a house built to last.

5. Uncle Leon Takes a Wife

In January 1954 at age forty-three, Uncle Leon married a widow lady, Bessie Lomax. I remember him showing us a picture of her in a magazine for people searching for a companion. I think I recall, 'a lonely-hearts club' mentioned. I was only three when they married. I have vague glimpses, not extended memories from age three. I suppose any time a memory is recollected at age three, no matter the length, it is quite remarkable.

Aunt Bessie lived in Ninety-Six, SC, and of course Daddy took Uncle Leon there to meet and court Aunt Bessie. I don't remember Uncle Leon ever driving a car or owning one but he did pay for gas and even helped Daddy pay for the car.

I have no idea how long their courtship lasted, but not long, I'm sure. Maybe they wrote each other letters, which would have been the only way to communicate in our neck of the woods in the early '50s. We didn't have telephones back then.

In the summer of 1954 there was a brick flue built on the outside of the large part of the house for the back bedroom to be converted into another kitchen. This became our kitchen. The original two rooms were again blocked off from the rest of the house, so Bessie and Leon could have their own place. A piece of linoleum covered the door opening on our side; Aunt Bessie had curtains to cover the opening in their apartment with her dresser in front of the curtains. Per Uncle Leon's notepad he carried, he and Bessie begin keeping house to themselves on September 6, 1954. He probably had to make arrangements for her comfort and their privacy before the actual move.

Uncle Leon and Aunt Bessie would use the original kitchen. He had purchased an electric stove in July 1953 while we still used the old one. I'm sure he had made up his mind he needed a lady companion and she would want a more modern stove.

We liked Aunt Bessie from the start and Uncle Leon loved her from the beginning. She had an infectious laugh and was always saying things we thought were funny. If she thought someone was smart, she would say, "He's a 'clever' little person." She also was good at telling jokes, most of which I did not understand.

Whenever she strolled down to the outhouse, she took a roll of toilet tissue, bringing it back when she was finished. She always called the white, porcelain pee pot the "slop jar." It had a red rim, a bucket handle, and a cover. It was for nighttime use and was emptied every morning, otherwise it resided under the bed out of sight.

The original two rooms provided a private apartment for the newlyweds. Maybe Aunt Bessie stayed with one of her seven grown children until Uncle Leon made arrangements to accommodate her in the old house.

We had to have our own kitchen on our side of the house, which meant no access to indoor plumbing what-so-ever. We had a wash stand in the new kitchen and carried water in buckets from the outdoor spigot for cooking, bathing, dishwashing, and drinking. Filling the buckets in the afternoon was the job of me and my siblings. The buckets had to be filled every evening before dark.

The washstand Daddy built was about three feet high with a two-foot square top; the wooden legs angled outward. The table/washstand held a bucket of drinking water with a communal dipper, a wash pan, and bar of soap for hand washing. Above the washstand a shelf held two full buckets of water for other uses. We also had a kitchen table, built by Uncle Leon or Daddy and covered with a vinyl tablecloth. There was a long bench behind the table where all of the kids sat, my siblings and myself. There were wooden chairs for grown-ups, purchased, not homemade. I believe they were made from oak. There was an outward curve to the open back of each chair. The top piece had a scroll decoration and four or five dowels that fit into another piece at the bottom.

With the addition of Aunt Bessie to the house and the closing of the doorway between, I now had to cross the porch to visit Uncle Leon.

He and Aunt Bessie seemed to get along well and she was kind to us most of the time. I, however, thought she looked down on us and considered us to be noisy, rowdy children, which we were. Once Uncle Leon came outside when we were all swinging in a tree at the edge of the yard, and told us to quiet down because we were upsetting Aunt Bessie. That was the only time he ever chastised us for anything. Carrying her store-bought toilet tissue down to the outhouse and back when she was finished gave us a hint that she felt superior also. I realize now, she didn't dare leave it behind; she knew we would use it and she would have to buy more.

We never bought toilet tissue on the roll that I remember. We did however use the Sears and Roebuck catalog. It not only gave us something entertaining to look at, but it worked pretty well for clean-up. We kids never thought twice about using the catalog pages to clean our bottoms. We didn't use corncobs like the image perpetuated of poor southern farmers of that period. The door of our outhouse also did not have a cut-out of a half-moon on the door, another stereotype. In every picture, cartoon, or otherwise, when outhouses were shown the half- moon is there. I never understood that significance. Ventilation, I'm sure, but why the half-moon?

Aunt Bessie's children in Ninety-Six lived in what seemed to us fancy brick houses. Actually, they were mill houses and every one of them was almost identical in size and layout. They weren't really rich, just above us in material status. Those things didn't mean they were any better, but I believe they thought they were.

6. Excited About School

Once, before I was old enough to go to school, on a special day, the students were allowed to bring their little brother or sister with them to school to find out what it was like. Kinda like, "take your kid or parent to work with you to understand your job day." Lula Mae was in the second grade and Louise was in the fourth. I remember sitting in the desk with Lula Mae in Mrs. Derrick's class. She was such a nice lady, small and slender, head completely covered with grey curls, glasses perched on her nose. I thought she was terribly old, probably over fifty. Gasp! I wish I were that age now. To a little five-year-old the teacher was a formidable authority figure. She had a squeaky little voice and was so kind to all the kids. I sat at the desk with Lula Mae while the students were working on an exercise. I got so sleepy, Mrs. Derrick said it was okay if I lay my head on the desk to rest. Guess what, pretty soon my sister lay her head down and fell asleep with me. The other half of the day, I spent with Louise in her classroom, also sitting with her. I don't remember anything special except I thought she was in the big kids' class and every one of her friends thought I was such a cute baby. Of course, there were other little brothers and sisters visiting with their older siblings, too. We liked school so much back then that was one thing we did in the summer to entertain ourselves. We played school.

"Well, when I was your age," Uncle Leon would say, "I had to walk three miles to school no matter how cold or rainy it was. Kids nowadays don't have to do that. Y'all have it so easy."

I thought, but of course didn't say: *we still had to get up before sunrise when even the birds were still asleep. We would get dressed, eat our grits and ride a bus for over an hour, stopping dozens of times to pick up students. It was, after all, fifteen miles to school.*

Actually, riding that bus was the best part of the whole experience, except for recess. I always sat beside Nancy and we became great friends. The bus drivers then were senior boys or girls, not adults like today.

I started first grade in Miss Iva Garvin's class. She was a tall, foreboding figure who didn't smile often and ran our class like the military. When she said do something, she meant now: walk in a straight line, stop talking to each other, and repeat the alphabet were all commands, not merely requests. We were really scared of her, at least I was. We had to take a blanket to school for nap time. She would sit at her desk and read while we quietly lay on our blankets and kept silent.

We all marched to the lunchroom together, lined up to pick up our tray from the lunch ladies and sat together at tables, with Miss Garvin at the head of the table to make sure there were no lapses in behavior. Lunch cost $1.00 per week and the food was good. I really liked rainy days. We had vegetable soup and sandwiches, pimento cheese or peanut butter mixed with honey. I always asked for half pimento cheese and half peanut butter. Of course, this included a glass bottle of milk. The milk was three cents a bottle, but the one-dollar weekly total covered that, too.

I found out that Miss Garvin was not so scary after all. I came in from recess, hot and red faced. All the children had to burn off some of that pent-up energy and it was quite normal to be red-faced. I must have been especially so and she was concerned. She sat me on her lap and fanned me with one of those cardboard fans with the flat stick attached to the back. The same fans we used at church with Bible verses and Jesus on the front, and an advertisement for the local funeral home on the back. Why did they need to advertise? There was always someone dying to use their business. Just a touch of humor I heard from some of my grownups.

I have to say here before I forget. When I was a kid, there were no ambulances to call or emergency 911. If you needed to be carried to the hospital, you called the funeral home and they came to pick you up in a hearse. So, I have already had one ride in the back of a hearse. I'm in no hurry to have another.

Back to impressions of first grade. Down the hall between the first and second grade classrooms was the girls' bathroom. The boys' bathroom was on another hall. I only mention the bathroom because that was another experience all together. We had a bathroom break before we went to lunch. All the girls lined up in a straight line in the hallway. Once we were allowed in the bathroom, we were allowed to talk. The first cubical had a door and a sign "Teachers Only." They had a latch on the inside so they had some privacy. We children had none at all. There were four or five cubicles with a commode in each, but no doors. When it was your turn to sit down on the commode, there were two girls standing on either side in the same cubicle, making it really hard to relax and time was of the essence. You had to take care of business and hop up so the next girl could sit down. There was a row of sinks on the wall and, of course, we were required to wash our hands when finished. As you can imagine that did not always happen. I hated the bathroom drill.

After I had been in first grade about six weeks, we got our 1st report to take home and be signed by one of our parents. This same report card was used all year and would be sent home and returned signed.

My Momma Sallie signed that first report card, and then she was gone.

7. Our Momma Was Beautiful

When I was small, I remember my mother, Sallie, as a beautiful woman. She had long black hair with a little curl on the top. Her complexion was dark as if she had a perfect tan. She wore makeup, not out of necessity. Her complexion was almost flawless except for the little black mole on the right above her ruby lips. Actually, it was considered a beauty mark. Many Hollywood actresses in the fifties added a beauty mark with a black pencil. Momma's was natural. Her eyes were very dark brown, almost black and twinkled when she smiled. We children loved her very much and were proud of her appearance.

Momma told my sister Louise how she met my father. Momma was only fourteen, right after World War II and Daddy's "Crazy Band" was playing at Uncle Eugene and Aunt Ethel's home near where Momma Sallie was living with her grandparents, Milledge and Lizzie Hartley. After I became an adult, I did have a relationship with Momma and she told me that Grandma Lizzie only wanted her to live with them so she could cook, iron, and clean up behind Lizzie's six sons living at home. She said when she first moved to Grandma Lizzie's to help her with chores, she was just a child and had to stand on a chair to iron clothes, cook, and wash dishes. She got tired of being Grandma Lizzie's servant. I think her unhappiness of that situation may have been the main reason she had married Daddy so young.

***

I remember Momma helping Grandma Florence wash clothes and cook. Washing clothes was done the same way it had been done for years. At least there was a spigot in the backyard now, no carrying water from the spring. I can remember this wash day process and it was absolutely an all-day job for Grandma and Momma. The cleaned and rinsed clothes were hung on the clothes lines to the left of the pump house. My daddy's white shirts were submerged in a pan of water with a goodly amount of Niagara starch added. Squeezed and twisted to wring out the water, they were also hung on the clothesline. When dry they were "stiff as a board" and ready to be sprinkled with water, rolled up, then ironed. There was a Pepsi bottle with a silver stopper filled with holes, like a salt shaker, used to dampen the clothes for ironing. The ironing part was another all-day job, no permanent press then.

Momma Sallie was a worker, a big help to Grandma. I'm sure Grandma appreciated Sallie's help, but she also seemed a little jealous probably because Robert was her only son. Uncle Eugene, Grandma's brother, did say Florence was bossy when she was younger. She was the oldest of eleven children, twenty-five years older than the youngest, Aunt Rosalee.

There might have been some tension there between Grandma and Momma Sallie. Momma had been bossed enough by her Grandma Lizzie and wasn't going to let her mother-in-law tell her exactly what to do. There was never any discord between the two in front of us kids.

After a wash day, I noticed Momma's long blue chenille housecoat hanging on the clothes line to dry. It had blue swirls and pink flowers in between the swirls. I know it must have been a favorite of hers. She always loved pretty clothes, jewelry, and shoes. These things she never got living with her grandparents.

We kids thought that long blue housecoat could be draped across two clothes lines and with enough clothes pins would become a neat hammock for us to climb into. This little escapade may have included only Steve and me, I don't remember, but we did put her nice long chenille robe across two lines and snap clothes pins all the way on both sides, and then climbed in. The pins popped off and we tumbled to the ground, rolling down the incline towards the terrace. We were kids. We could have rolled all the way to the spring and got up laughing. We were tough and never thought of breaking a bone. The fancy robe wasn't torn, thankfully. She would have been furious.

***

Momma went to work at the sewing room in Pelion, after all her children were born. She would have been, at least, twenty-two at that time. Pelion was the same community where we would attend school. She rode to work with someone, Aunt Binnie, I think. She and daddy both were gone to work early in the morning leaving Grandma in charge of us kids.

I can remember Momma coming home from work late in the evening and talking about her wonderful boss, Mr. Hightower, and how good he was to her. I didn't understand adult relationships then, but looking back, Mr. Hightower probably had a hidden agenda behind his kindness. Momma was very attractive. She thought so too. I could see she had a high opinion of her charms. Probably Mr. Hightower and others had planted that seed in her mind, and she became vain, at times putting her wants above her husband and children. She was so young when she married my daddy, she was most probably overwhelmed by the attention and compliments other men gave to her. I know it made her feel good about herself and encouraged her to take pride in her appearance.

In Uncle Leon's little book, he says, "Sallie showed herself and took Kathy to Coley's, her father, on Sunday March 31, 1957. She came back from Coley's on Wednesday, April 3, 1957." It was evident she was not happy or satisfied with her life. Leaving on a whim for days, and not telling my daddy when she would be back happened on more than one occasion according to my older sisters.

I don't remember her taking me, but I can remember one dark night we stood beside the highway and she was holding me. Grandpa Coley had left home drunk, "high as a Georgia pine," Uncle Leon would say. He was alone and had run off the highway into a field. We were standing by the wreck site. Grandpa was not in the car and Grandma Sara Bell was not concerned. I really don't think she was too worried about his injuries. Evidently, they had a terrible row before he took off in the car. She was in no hurry to locate him.

All I remember is Momma was holding me. It was dark and I had on a winter dress coat with a black velveteen collar that felt so soft and nice. The coat is the reason I probably remember and also Momma holding me. I have no other memory of her holding me or even sitting on her lap.

I accidentally overheard Grandma say once that Momma went to see Dr. Williams in Wagener because he gave her "that old dope." We were little kids; I only noticed how hard she was to please and that she didn't smile or laugh as often. I had no idea at the time what Grandma's comment about my Momma's visits to Dr. Williams implied. Thinking back, it must have been some narcotic she referred to. I never remember seeing Momma smoke or drink alcohol and she never smelled of either. She always smelled of "Evening in Paris."

If she had an addiction, it had to be to pills, "that old dope" that Grandma mentioned with such disgust when she thought we were nowhere around. I knew something was up. Our Grandma was the kindest, most gentle person I can remember. She was never one to say a bad thing about a soul and never given to gossip. Maybe she knew Sallie wasn't treating daddy or us the way she should.

Lula Mae said, "Momma left more than one time she could recall. Once Momma came into the back yard and told daddy she wanted to take the car."

He said, "No," so she threw the car keys at him. This I don't remember. I'm sure my older sisters remember things differently than I do. After she went to work her whole personality seemed to change and not for the better, where we children were concerned.

8. Abandoned

I don't remember the exact date, but it was late October, 1957. The weather had not yet gotten cold; maybe it was what the old folks called Indian Summer. It was a very dark night and the heavy wooden door was open, and the light on the porch was on. We heard a car horn blow. The car stopped in the road in front of our house. Opening the screen door, we kids peeped out and saw the bright tail lights. We thought nothing special about it until Momma pushed us aside, ran out the door and down the steps, and headed behind the car shed and into the cornfield. We watched as the car slowly crawled up the road towards Rayflin and stopped briefly on the rise at the place my daddy intended to build our family a new house. When the car stopped evidently Momma climbed in; it disappeared on down the road.

We kids did not need any explanation. We knew our momma had left us, and we all started to cry. Four little dirty faced ragamuffins, ages four, six, eight and ten.

She didn't even look back, say goodbye or acknowledge us in any way. She just rushed by us. No "see you soon," or "I love you," or even a backward glance as she crossed the porch. She was running barefoot, getting away as fast as she could. She had a grand plan and her young children were not part of it.

My siblings probably remember that night differently, but the result was the same: our mother was gone and did not intend to return.

The next day Daddy and Uncle Leon traced her path across the field of dry corn stalks. The foot prints were deep and wide a part. She was definitely running. She had crossed the cornfield, the stream at Coon Branch, and up the rise to the new house site where the mysterious car picked her up. We had no clue where she went. My daddy eventually found out with whom and where she had gone, but never shared it with us kids growing up. In fact, Daddy never said anything against our momma to us kids.

A couple of weeks later, Momma came to my classroom door. Miss Garvin, my first-grade teacher, had us lined up for some reason, I don't remember why. When I saw Momma, I ran to her and wrapped my arms around her legs. I was so happy to see her, that's all I remember. She was working near the school, but I can't speculate on why she decided to come by that day. I know she had to come to the house to pick up her clothes and things, but I don't recall when or how many times, either. Maybe my young mind blocked out the actual visits to take away her things, it would have made it more final. It possibly was only once.

Daddy tried to talk Momma into coming home when she came to the house. I only remember one time she was there. I was sitting on the bed with her in their old bedroom and Daddy was talking to her. I'm not sure what he said, but I actually told him not to say that to her and he popped my cheek. I was taking up for her. The slap was not hard, but it shocked me more than anything and hurt only my feelings. My daddy just did not do that sort of thing. Whatever the circumstances of that one time, I was too young to understand their conflict. I guess I took up for her because, from a child's point of view, I loved her and felt Daddy was being too harsh. When I was in the fifth grade, they divorced.

Daddy had to get a lawyer and his lawyer was a cousin, Floyd Spence. Floyd later served eighteen years as a U.S. Congressman from South Carolina. Uncle Leon use to say, "Floyd's Mammie ran an elevator in one of those big tall buildings in Columbia and his Pa, Jim Spence, ran a trolley car," proof you don't have to be born with a silver spoon in your mouth to make something of yourself. Daddy did get custody of all us children, which back then that was very uncommon. Floyd might have been that good of a lawyer; it's more likely, I think, that Momma didn't want custody.

At Christmas the first year she was gone, Momma sent Aunt Binnie to our house with bags of toys. We opened them on the porch. I don't think they were wrapped and don't remember if they had our names on them or if we just picked out what we wanted. Perhaps the gifts were just a way to soothe her conscious about leaving.

Grandma became our anchor. She was seventy years old when my Momma deserted us. Grandma was the only person there for us. She knew Daddy's job at the cotton mill fed and clothed us, she was the one who cooked and tried to keep us safe when he couldn't be there. It was a sad situation especially for the '50s. No other child in my class came from a "broken home." They all had a mother who lived with them, but no mother could have done better than Grandma. She had the patience of Job, was good to us, and kept us out of too much mischief. She did the best she could to take care of four rambunctious children.

9. Things Change in the Old House

After our momma didn't come back, Grandma completely took over our care. I now slept in the bed with her, Lula Mae and Lousie slept in the other double bed. Steve slept in a twin bed that had once belonged to Cousin Tony in the room with daddy.

In the winter, our bedroom was very cold. We spent most of our time after dark in our new kitchen where it was warm. On winter mornings, we would grab our clothes and run to the kitchen to get dressed behind the wood stove where it was warm. The wood stove was a huge oval cast iron stove which stood up on legs, with a brown metal sheet under it. It had a long pipe that went out from the top rear of the stove, bending way above our heads and inserting in the chimney flue outside the kitchen, so the smoke could escape. It was a nice warm place, behind that stove for dressing. On either side of that stove there was chrome-coated attachments where we could prop our feet to warm them without actually touching the fiery cast iron. Of course, we didn't prop bare feet on the chrome; we still needed shoes for protection. Daddy got the fire going before he went to work in the cotton mill. When we got up, there was only Grandma to see that we were fed and ready to go. Back then families had only one car, and maybe an old truck or a tractor for planting. Like everyone else, we only had the one car, a gray 1950 Ford purchased the 20th of August 1955 per Uncle Leon's notes. My daddy was always a Ford man.

Grandma, bless her heart, always made sure we had breakfast. Every school morning, we had hot grits and butter for breakfast, sometimes with fried fat back. On special occasions, we had cheese to mix into those grits and, of course, homemade biscuits. We would hear the bus careening down the dirt road, a loud rumbling, from the south, and we'd grab our books and head for the door. All the high school senior drivers drove the yellow monster as fast as it could go. There was something called "governors" that only allowed the bus to go a certain speed, a good thing I suppose looking back.

Winter time in the old house, we spent our time in the kitchen since it had the wood heater and was the only warm room in the house. First, we had a Home Comfort wood cook stove: there was a reservoir on the left side that was filled with water. Whenever there was a fire in the cook stove the water stayed hot, handy for making instant coffee, washing dishes, or adding to bathe water. Grandma loved her coffee and added lots of evaporated milk. We didn't take all-over baths in the winter but did wash our feet before turning in for the night.

We did our homework at the kitchen table while Grandma cooked supper. We sometimes watched TV, but on school nights we had to be in bed pretty early. It was cold in our bedroom, with no heat of any kind, so we would jump in bed under a mountain of quilts. As a young child, I could hardly turn over because the quilts were so heavy and I was so small. If I did attempt to turn over, Grandma would immediately say, "Quit fanning the cover." Lifting the covers caused a draft of cold air to flood underneath.

The old house was not insulated. Sometimes the window panes rattled in the wind. There was nothing between us and the outside, no Venetian blinds or even long curtains, just the window panes. If a glass of water was left on Grandma's dresser, sometimes there would be a film of ice on top of the water the next morning.

I was trapped under that mountain of quilts, some of which belonged to my great grandmother. Quilts were never thrown away, only repurposed, used instead of cotton batting inside a new quilt. I would shiver in my little nest until my body heat warmed a cocoon, and then I did not move all night. Once I got a warm spot I stayed there. One advantage to sleeping with Grandma was she had an electric heating pad or maybe it was a brick heated in the fire than wrapped in a towel, but it was to warm her feet. I would scrooch down until I had my icy little feet on grandma's heat source, and we would share.

We had more snow and ice when I lived there compared to when I was older. The icicles would hang from the eaves of the house and the smokehouse at least ten to twelve inches long. We loved when it snowed and actually prayed it would. If the snow was deep enough Grandma would send us outside to get a bowl of clean snow and she would make snow ice cream. We had never heard of acid rain or pollution.

Snowy days were always the best, no school. There was no way a school bus could make it down to our house and most of the children in our school were country kids that lived on dirt roads.

Winter was my favorite time of year, not because it was cold, but Christmas was finally getting close. We always hoped for a white Christmas, but we never got one.

By mid-October every year, we children had devotedly searched the woods for the perfect Christmas tree; it had to be a cedar. Anytime we were in the woods playing, we always had our eyes open for just the right one. When we found it, we would tell Daddy.

About two weeks before Christmas we would tramp through the woods with daddy to present it to him. He would cut it down with a bow saw and drag it back to the house. We were so excited; we skipped and hopped along or tried to help carry the tree. If we put our hands on the tree, they were bound to get some sticky sap on them; it was not easy to remove, but we didn't care. Christmas always seemed so far away when I was growing up. For kids Christmas never came around fast enough. It seems like that still to children, but then in the '50s we only got toys at Christmas. Presents were frivolous unnecessary indulgences other than during the holidays.

10. Christmas Memories

My first memories were of the living room, seldom used, except at Christmas time. In the winter, especially at Christmas, Daddy built a fire in the living room fireplace and kept it going through the holidays. If I close my eyes I can still sense the wonderful smell of burning cedar. Daddy always had to trim a few branches off the Christmas tree and they were thrown into the fireplace. This fireplace contained what was then called fire dogs, basically cast-iron rods with two feet front and back with an ornamental front piece. The purpose was to hold the larger pieces of wood placed above the beginning fire of splinters and dry wood. There was a cast iron fire poker propped against the side of the mantelpiece to stir and poke the fire when necessary.

There were only two closets in the whole house, one in the old dining room next to the original kitchen and one in the living room. I suspect that closet in the living room was the repository for our gifts Santa brought. He sure could get in and out like a ghost. Behind this fireplace was Momma and Daddy's room with another fireplace. They were both separate but vented somehow up the same brick chimney.

Daddy would put our tree in the tree stand. It may have

held a cup of water and had to be replenished daily. He always strung the big colored electric bulbs on the tree, then we kids were in charge of decorating. We would add the ball ornaments; all would be antiques now. The silver and colored garlands were next and finally the silver icicles that we would try to string from each branch as if they were dripping off the tree. That soon got old, trying to place each one separately, so we would toss handfuls on the branches. Always ready to chide our other siblings about what would look better, there was normally a discussion about what each one was doing wrong.

"Steve you have the balls too close together on the branches, spread further apart," Louise would say. "We want it to be beautiful and not all cluttered and messy." He paid her no attention whatsoever, and she and Lu sometimes redecorated his section.

"Leave my balls where I hung them," he would warn. "I know what looks good, girls are such a pain, just a bunch of know-it-alls."

When the decorating was done, we would rush outside to see how beautiful it looked from the front window. The only other Christmas decoration we had was a small crinkled red cellophane wreath, with a red bulb on a short socket in the middle and a silver cut-out with Merry Christmas written on it. This always went in the window behind the tree.

Grandma was in the kitchen cooking on our now electric stove. She thought it was a wonder; it replaced the old wood-burning Home Comfort stove. Christmas was a time of making pies, cakes, especially a huge fruitcake and other sweet treats. Daddy would buy boxes of fruit, oranges, apples, and bananas. By the time Christmas was over we kids were on sugar overload.

One year a couple of weeks before Christmas, Burlington Mill, where daddy worked, had a Christmas giveaway for all the employees' children. Daddy took all four of us. I remember we sat on metal bleachers and the children lined up to receive their gift bags from the company. They had big white handled shopping bags with Santa Claus on the side. The boys and girls bags were different. We thought we had really won the jackpot. There were coloring books, crayons, paddle-balls, kaleidoscopes, jack stones, fruit, and candy. I can't remember what else was in the girls' bag, but all the kids were overwhelmed. I think there may have been one of those red net stockings with candy and little toys. They were real popular in the '50s and I do remember we all had one. We were determined to hang them on our tree. The only problem was they were too heavy. We turned the tree over several times before we gave up on that idea.

Now it was Christmas Eve. Santa always came to our house on Christmas Eve, that's when we got our presents. We were stuck in the kitchen with Grandma while she cooked the turkey. It was cooked on the top of the stove in a dishpan with another turned down over it. I know this because Lula Mae got a camera for Christmas one year and took a picture of Grandma standing in front of the stove while the turkey was cooking in the background.

We had to stay in the kitchen so Santa Claus could deliver our presents. Uncle Leon was just as excited as us about Christmas. He showed us sled marks on the ground outside below the living room window; he swore they were made by Santa's sleigh.

The door to the living room was closed so Santa would be able to sneak in and deliver our toys. We took turns every five or ten minutes sneaking down the hall to peek into the living room to see if Santa had been there. There is no way he could have gotten past us, we checked so often, but somehow he did. Our presents were not wrapped but were in separate piles, so we knew which ones belonged to who. Actually, we got a lot for Christmas. I always got a doll, usually a game, and several other things. We all made a list and Santa tried to bring what we asked for.

Daddy said when he was a boy his Christmas was in a shoe box, a cap pistol with caps, an orange, an apple, a handful of nuts, and some hard candy. Imagine what the kids today would think of that. We were not wealthy but all the kids we knew pretty much led the same kind of life. In fact, we probably appeared rich to some of our schoolmates.

Santa would even come to our back kitchen window by the stove before Christmas and ask what we wanted. Louise and Lula Mae would talk to him while Steve and I would hide under the table and refuse. Grandma said I wasn't going to get anything from Santa because I cut all the pictures of toys out of the Christmas catalog and Santa didn't like me doing that. When and if he did appear, I would hide all my clippings under the kitchen cabinet. I was afraid Santa would see them.

Years later when we were much older, we found out our mysterious Santa was Uncle Leon.

Just to clarify, even though Uncle Leon was married to Aunt Bessie, she was gone a lot. She was a widow when they married in '54 and some of her adult children, I think she had seven, were often coming to pick her up. They might keep her for six months at a time, and then she was brought home. I don't know if she even wrote Uncle Leon letters while she was away. She would be gone for months on end and then just reappear one day. Uncle Leon was very close to us kids. Being thirteen years older than Daddy, he almost seemed like a granddaddy to us.

11. Thick as Thieves

Uncle Leon always made me feel special. Almost every morning I would cross the porch to their part of the house, knock on the door, and he would open it with a smile and shaving cream on his face.

"Good morning, Skeeter," he would say. "Isn't it about time for the bus?"

"I'm ready. Just wanted to tell you goodbye."

Then he would reach in his pocket and give me a nickel, dime, or quarter. "Buy yourself an ice cream or drink at school."

"Gee, thanks. See you this afternoon," I would toss over my shoulder as I ran to the hall door.

Back in the '50s a nickel, dime, or quarter would buy a lot at school. Ice creams were sold at recess by the school janitor, Mr. Crouch. They were a nickel or dime each depending on which you wanted. Mr. Crouch sat on a stool beside a chest freezer, you handed him the money through the window, and he gave you your ice cream.

Coca-Colas were available in glass bottles for ten cents; a pack of cookies or peanuts was a nickel. For some reason it was all the rage to pour the peanuts in your drink. Another '50s thing kids did.

***

Uncle Leon did other special things for me, too. I can remember sitting on his lap in a rocking chair beside Aunt Bessie and watching President Eisenhower give a speech on the television. That was probably in 1956. Anyway, the General was our president and I believe the only politician Uncle Leon approved, probably because he had saluted the General on more than one occasion during World War II. Uncle Leon called Nixon "Tricky Dick" and Clinton "Slick Willie", not especially titles of approval. I don't know if he voted in elections. Probably not.

He and I developed a special friendship; we were buddies. Knowing how much I enjoyed catching butterflies, he made me a special butterfly catcher. It was basically a window screen box, two inches on the four sides with a screen bottom. There was a long flat handle attached to the bottom of the screen. It worked great to trap the butterflies.

Aunt Bessie dumped her dishwater out the back window, so the ground was always moist and attracted many butterflies. Mostly the little grey-blue ones, but also some yellow or orange monarch butterflies. I would catch them with my screen net, put them in a jar with holes in the lid, take them inside our bedroom, push the window up, and free them. I would then lower the window and trap them between the window and the screen. I loved to watch them flit around, trapped so that I could observe them. Eventually, I'd let them go.

Aunt Bessie crocheted a lot, watched *Edge of Night* on TV, read *True Romance* magazines, and sometimes made little crafts. I remember she made me a small heart- shaped pillow with a blue crocheted cover and ruffles around the edge to match. It was for my birthday, just three days before Uncle Leon's, and I'm sure he asked her to make it. Another birthday he had Aunt Bessie make an arrangement of pink silk flowers in a white plastic cup.

When the weather turned cold, Uncle Leon set six or eight rabbit boxes. Every evening when the sun began to wane and darkness slowly crept over the land, I would accompany him to check them. We followed the little two-rut road beside the north field to the rise, then past the persimmon tree toward the trash pile. I can remember vividly, as we reached the rise I would look back towards the house, see the smoke bellowing from our kitchen chimney, and the orange sky in the background as the sun started to drop below the swamp. It was like a ritual to me: "looking back." I always did.' When we passed the persimmon tree, the ground underneath was always littered with fruit.

Uncle Leon would say, "I hope we don't have that old possum in one of the rabbit boxes." Then he'd warn me, "Never bite into a green persimmon. It will turn your mouth inside out."

Of course, at six or seven years old, I wasn't so sure what "turn your mouth inside out" really meant. Children at that age usually take what old people say to have a literal meaning, so I tried to envision what that meant. Not being able to, I made no comment.

We would continue on the rabbit box trail. If the door of the box was down, there was something inside. Uncle Leon would stand the box on end and peek first. He didn't want to find a skunk, which could have been disastrous for both of us. In the South I grew up in, skunks were called pole cats. I don't have a clue why. If it was a rabbit in the box, he would reach down, find the rabbit's back legs, drag it out and with a quick chop to the back of the head, break the rabbit's neck. That meant rabbit and gravy for supper.

Once that old possum was in one of the boxes. Uncle Leon just opened the door, lay the box flat, and the possum waddled out and disappeared. I went with him every evening to check the boxes since I was four or five years old. It was something we both enjoyed. He wanted company and would tell me about plants and shared his wisdom. I didn't realize until much later how much he had taught me.

Once he took me on a very long walk. We walked most of the way on a two-rut road through the woods and crossed a couple of state-maintained dirt roads until we reached the highway where Uncle Willie, Grandma's brother, and Aunt Fannie lived. We visited them for a while and then walked home. Uncle Leon pretty much walked everywhere he went, mostly to visit relatives and I was his companion on many of these trips.

Uncle Leon had a little Bible that was sent to him by his father, Kelly, and Miss Florence, during World War II. It was made to fit in a soldier's left breast pocket and had a steel cover. On the cover it said, "May this keep you safe from harm", referring to the pocket it fit in over the soldier's heart. He gave it to me May 22, 1960, when I was nine years old. He wrote that in the front of the little Bible after his name "and I gave it to Kathy, May 22, 1960." It's the thing I treasure most. The fact that he gave it to me on Steve's birthday added to the fact that I was special to Uncle Leon.

He didn't attend church, but always sent his tithe by Daddy. He was not a big fan of crowds and I think he didn't feel worthy of regular church attendance. He had done such bad things in his past. He did, however, make exceptions for funerals. He felt that was important to honor the passing of friends and family. He never attended weddings. Years later when I married Jimmy, he amazingly attended ours. Of course, he wasn't at the reception; he sat in the car. Too many strange people, I guess.

There was an 8x10 colorized picture of me in first grade that sat in a frame on top of Uncle Leon's TV. I don't know who he got to add color. It was originally black and white. This would have been in 1957. Yep, I was his favorite.

12. Respect for our Elders, Television & Vices

Because high school seniors were the bus drivers, not adults, it was not the best or safest way to get to school. But I must say, for the most part, student drivers in the '50s and '60s were much more responsible and mature than high schoolers today. I'm sure that is true. We were taught respect at home. Parents said things like, "Stop crying or I'll give you something to cry about", "Children should be seen and not heard," and my particular favorite, "Because I said so."

We traveled in cars with no seat belts, no padded dashes, and no windows or doors, which could be locked by the driver for the safety of those in the back. Children in the back seat could open a window or door no matter the speed if they could not be locked. Of course, we knew better. Our parents were in charge and we never questioned their authority. We said ma'am and sir to all grownups when addressed directly. I taught my children the same respect and honesty I was taught. Car windows were always rolled completely down in warm weather and we knew better than to throw things out the window on purpose. I did enjoy laying on the seat and watching the electric lines appear to go up and down against the blue sky or float my hand out the window and feel the breeze pushing against my hand, which was like holding something cool and soft in my outstretched fingers.

***

The television was always tuned to the Friday night fights sponsored by Gillette. My daddy liked to watch them. We kids always loved westerns: *Wagon Train, Bronco, Cheyenne, Sugarfoot,* the *Rifleman,* and *Gunsmoke.* We also loved to sing along when the theme song came on introducing the show. Of course, we loved Clint Eastwood as Rowdy Yates in *Rawhide,* hearing the crack of the whip when driving the cattle was our favorite part of the "Rawhide" song. Nothing on television then was off limits for kids. It was nice to know, anything the grownups watched, we could too. The only thing, programs were in black and white, but then what you don't have, you don't miss, so black and white was great. We only had three channels, now way more than one hundred are available in most homes and there's nothing worth watching.

If we were ever up that late, the station would sign off at midnight with the *National Anthem* and then what looked like a dartboard was all that we could receive. Of course, there was that horrible buzzing sound, an announcement about what mega hertz the station operated on and when they would begin broadcasting again at seven a.m.

Saturday mornings were our favorite time for the television, cartoons and *Tarzan* movies. In the spring the television would be moved from the kitchen into the hall kinda catawampus beside the refrigerator. The refrigerator always sat in the hall. It just wouldn't fit in the kitchen. There was a folding screen placed behind the TV, white with bamboo leaves painted on it, no particular reason for the screen except aesthetic. It just looked better with the refrigerator concealed from the front door. We would then sit cross-legged on the floor for Saturday cartoons. That was the only time programming was really aimed at children. The television was in the kitchen in the winter because it was the only heated room; in spring and summer it was moved into the hall. It was never in the living room and of course there was only one television. I think the living room was strictly for visiting friends and neighbors, so that conversation, not television, was encouraged. The children were not expected to participate. We were normally sent outside to play, but you can imagine we heard a lot that was not intended for our ears.

There were lots of commercials on TV, but mostly a man would say, "We now pause for station identification." Very short, it was hardly an interruption of what we were watching. A commercial always had a mascot like: "Speedy" for Alka-Seltzer, "Tony the Tiger" for Frosted Flakes, the "Pillsbury dough boy," or the "Chiquita banana girl" with a hat covered in fruit. Another big seller for males was Brylcreem, with their motto, "A little dab will do you, they love to get their fingers in your hair." It practically guaranteed success with the ladies. Some high school boys thought "a little dab will do you" was the answer, but that was a load of garbage and besides it was quite greasy. That did not add to their appeal, but guess what folks, that's what we call targeting your audience.

All commercials had a little jingle and some were really catchy. The Kent cigarette commercial was my favorite. As with songs that introduced our favorite programs the song that introduced the western, *Sugarfoot*, was my favorite. We enjoyed the commercial jingles and these introductory theme songs almost as much as we did watching the characters in the programs. Back then kids could associate more with westerns because of their popularity on TV. My brother, Steve, always had a holster with toy pistols, Lincoln Logs to build a fort, and plastic cowboy and Indian figures.

As for cigarette commercials, kids could buy a box of candy cigarettes with red on the end for the fire, so we would pretend we were smoking. Most grown-ups smoked back then. We kids would pick what was called "rabbit tobacco" that grew wild in clearings and fallow fields, single stalks with slender gray leaves. We would strip the leaves, crumple them together, wrap them in strips of brown paper bag and pretend to smoke that. We may have even tried to light it; I'm pretty sure Steve did. We always took notice when Grandma's brothers, Eugene and James, rolled their own. They took out their cigarette papers, ripped one from the carboard holder, used their index finger to create a trough, and tapped the side of their red Prince Albert can to fill it. The finishing touch was to lick the edge of the paper so it would stick to the other side and a twist to each end so their tobacco wouldn't slide out. They had a perfect self-rolled cigarette, struck a match, and lit one end, puffing away.

Few men or women in the fifties were free from some form of

nicotine habit. At school, there was a smoking area outside where teenage boys gathered along with some teachers at recess to take a smoke break. Others chewed tobacco or dipped snuff. I do recall my Grandma Hartley always chewed tobacco. I had a couple of cousins on the Hartley side that smoked cigarettes or chewed tobacco and all sports coaches appeared to be chewing. Uncle Leon and Daddy always chewed tobacco. Uncle Leon carried a plug of Bull of the Woods in a small plastic bag and a plastic bottle with a screw top in his pocket to spit his juice in. He wouldn't just spit on the ground. Uncle Leon said the first time one of his uncles offered him a chew of tobacco, it made him so dizzy he thought he was going to fall off the world.

Grandma Florence didn't have any vices that I know of. She didn't drink alcohol, use any tobacco products, or spout any of that "blackguard talk" as she called curse words. I don't mean to imply she was saintly, none of us are and she could be right bossy at times. Even her brothers attested to that.

***

Children were more respectful back then. We knew we should be seen and not heard. Interrupting grown up conversation was both rude and disrespectful, not that we were not absorbing everything that they said. We did what we were told and kept our opinions to ourselves, otherwise Daddy might use his belt or a switch on our legs or bottoms. I got very few whippings when I was bad, besides I had enough sense to know that when I did, I deserved it. It was definitely not child abuse. As it states in the *Bible*, "spare the rod and spoil the child."

13. Weekend Traditions — Building & Church

My daddy bought ten acres from Aunt Jennie, Granddaddy Kelly's sister, in 1956, adjacent to Uncle Leon's property. He began clearing it off before Mamma left, thinking we needed our own house and that it would please her.

He had a pump put down and Uncle Leon built a small cement block house with a shingled roof to protect it from the cold. An electric service pole with meter was also put on the site for a light in the little block house and daddy would have electricity for other building needs, saws, and lights to work. Daddy had an old wooden trailer with a two-wheel axel. He would buy about twenty or more blocks every payday. He also bought materials, gravel, sand, and bags of cement to mix up the mortar used to lay blocks. The gravel and sand had to be delivered by dump truck. He accumulated his materials until he thought he had enough to start building. He had never laid cement block before but was smart enough to figure it out. He actually began building in the fall of 1958.

As a small child, second grade, I guess, I can remember when he dug the trenches all around where the walls would be built. The trenches would be filled with cement, forming the foundation where the outside block walls would be laid. I can remember playing in the piles of dirt thrown from the trench. If he had help, it would have been Uncle Leon or Grandma's brothers, Eugene and James. He didn't have a blueprint, but I remember he did measure carefully and made sure everything was level. He used what was called a chalk line in a silver metal container. A thick string wound inside had a little silver ring to pull it out. Anytime he wanted to measure a straight line, he would have someone hold the container close to the floor, pull the silver ring until he had reached the place where the line was to go. He would then pluck the string which resulted in a straight line marked by purple chalk. One of us kids usually held the metal container for daddy to measure.

He borrowed an electric cement mixer from a Mr. Jeffcoat. Sand, gravel, and cement was shoveled into the mixer, water added and switched on. As it rotated, the ingredients were mixed thoroughly then dumped in the trench for the foundation. Many times, the mixer was emptied and refilled. The block would be laid on the foundation after it set up for days. All of this cement had to be level. How my daddy did that, I have no clue, but like all the Gantts, he was good at building and he found a way.

***

On Sundays he took me and my siblings to Sunday school and

preaching at Steadman Baptist Church. We were all neatly dressed in church clothes. I can remember how boring the sermons were, and I usually lay down on the pew and dozed off. It seemed like two hours, but to a kid, a "hell and brimstone" Baptist preacher could interrupt your nap. We all knew to be quiet and behave, no question about that. My daddy took us every Sunday, since Grandma didn't attend morning service. Sometimes she would go at night for what we called Training Union. She had a badly bent back from osteoporosis and had to sit at the end of a pew with her back sort of in the corner in order to be reasonably comfortable. Pews were not padded then at all and it had to be very painful for our little Grandma. The entire twenty-two years she was with me, she never weighed over one hundred pounds. Her height was less than five feet. I thought when I was very small, *if I could be as tall as Grandma, I would be happy.* Before she left us, I was way taller and I'm only five feet two inches. Anyway, I guess morning service was too crowded. Besides, she would have our Sunday dinner ready when we got home and we were always starving after a long sermon.

We looked forward to Sunday dinners and usually had company or we would go visit some of our family afterwards. Most Sundays, Grandma made fried chicken, rice and gravy, macaroni and cheese, and always homemade biscuits. We had homemade biscuits or corn bread at every meal.

Daddy bought a twenty-five-pound bag of flour a week and it was dumped in a red metal Pepsi Cola barrel kept under Grandma's cook table in the kitchen. Once the flour was dumped in the Pepsi barrel, the bags were reused. In the '50s, flour sacks were made from cloth. The seams were carefully clipped until it was one flat piece of material, then washed, ironed, and could be used to make clothing. I don't have any idea the size of a twenty-five-pound flour sack when spread out and pressed. Lots of kids had clothes made from the sack cloth. It was cotton material usually with a floral pattern. I had a dress made from flour sacks. I don't know how many it may have taken, probably more than one. My dress was white with little blue flowers. There is a picture of me about age six standing beside Grandma's rose bush with my homemade flour sack dress on, adorned with blue bias tape sewn around a square neck and about two inches above the hem.

Sunday was always considered a day of rest when I grew up in the old house. In the '50s, it was considered a sin to cut grass, fish, or plow your fields. Unless "the ox is in the ditch" you were supposed to honor the day. Folks just didn't work on Sunday; it was considered the Lord's Day. That was the way we Baptists interpreted the scripture. Stores were closed and people were off work. It was a day to spend with your family. Today it is just considered the weekend, stores are open and people have to work. Sunday in the '50s was considered a day to visit with your family and friends. The only time now I see extended family is at funerals. Sad, but so true.

14. Southern Fried

Almost everything Grandma cooked was fried in pure lard. It came in green and white waxed boxes at the grocery store or we were given lard by some of the kin folks that had butchered a hog.

Having been born in the Victorian era and living as tenant farmers, Grandma didn't waste any food. If there was leftover rice, she made rice pudding; left over biscuits, she made bread pudding. Grandma made everything from scratch. She usually made dessert, a layer cake, fried apple pies, or banana pudding. She never measured ingredients. Very seldom did she consult a printed recipe; if so, it was probably from the Home Comfort cookbook that came with the wood cook stove.

The meat we ate was chicken, pork chops, beef liver, and chicken livers, or rabbits and squirrels daddy killed in the woods or Uncle Leon caught in his boxes. Of course, it was all fried, the drippings used for gravy. The biscuits were often used to sop gravy if there was no rice, potatoes, or grits to mix it in. We also had a lot of fried fish, fried vegetables like yellow squash, okra, or Daddy's favorite fried green tomatoes. The squash, okra, and green tomatoes were battered before placing in the hot lard. The only thing Grandma cooked that I despised was her beef liver.

She didn't, for some reason, make gravy with that and it was hard and overly crispy. I never voiced my objection. I knew better.

We always ate lots of pure cane syrup. It came in big can with a top that had to be pried off like a paint can. I watched Uncle Leon many nights at the supper table put a pat of butter on his plate, pour cane syrup on it, flatten with his fork, then sop it with a biscuit. I guess that was his dessert when nothing else was available. Daddy bought canned salmon for Grandma to make fried salmon patties or a huge can of Prairie Belt sausage, still available in dollar stores and Wal Mart in small cans. The picture of the little boy in the striped shirt hasn't changed since I was a child. Aunt Jemima and Betty Crocker may have been upgraded, but not the Prairie Belt kid. The can of sausage Grandma used must have been gallon size; when opened all those little sausages were swimming in grease. Grandma took a fork, fished out enough to heat in the iron skillet, and the rest was covered and placed in the refrigerator for later. There was also something called tripe that came in a can. Grandma would rake the congealed fat off, flour, and fry the tripe. I ate it, but it was tough and chewy. It didn't taste bad and no grown-up told us what it really was. I didn't know at the time, it was cow stomach.

The best thing, palate wise, was real cream and hot biscuits. Growing up we never used such a fancy word as palate when talking about a special taste. Sometimes, we would get a pint of that wonderful thick cream from Miss Estelle or Miss Fannie. It was extremely rich, having been skimmed off of the top of fresh cows' milk. When I lived in the old house, we had no domestic animals: cow, mule, pigs, or chickens. The barn was torn down before I was born or shortly thereafter.

Uncle Leon always had a vegetable garden down near the spring, so fresh vegetables were available in the summer. What we didn't eat, Grandma preserved by canning in glass fruit jars with a pressure cooker. I only took part in the process of shelling peas or butter beans or picking squash, tomatoes, and cucumbers. If we picked a basket of butter beans or peas, they had to be shelled right away. If not, newspaper was spread on the floor and the vegetables were dumped and spread out. Leaving them in the basket overnight or for several hours would cause them to go through a heat, which meant they would collect moisture and would go bad. Uncle Leon always planted a row of carrots. When they were matured, we kids would pull them up, wipe off the sand, and eat them raw. We also ate red tomatoes off the vine. I'm fairly sure as a child, I ate a goodly amount of dirt.

We also ate lots of potatoes, both white and sweet potatoes. Grandma would cook the 'iced' potatoes in water till tender then add lots of butter and canned evaporated milk. It was years before I realized when someone said 'iced' potatoes they were really saying Irish potatoes, just the way Southerners pronounced the word.

Reminds me of comments I have received about my southern speech. Once years later at a Daughters of the American Revolution convention in Washington, D.C., when I got in the elevator at the Capitol Hilton and politely asked some gentlemen to mash the 3rd floor button, he replied, "Is that mash as in Georgia or South Carolina?"

"That would be South Carolina," I replied.

I just can't hide where I'm from, not that I want to. On a trip to Canada, before crossing the Canadian border pass Orville,

Washington, we stopped at a duty-free liquor store. When I went to pay, the guy at the cash register said, "You're not from around here are you?"

I answered him, "Do you think? What gave it away?" I smiled, "Just teasing. I'm from South Carolina."

The cashier gave me a big smile, "I couldn't help but notice that southern accent."

Back to the foods we ate growing up. My grandma made sassafras tea, especially in the winter. She made this mostly for herself because she liked it, but we kids never did. There were plenty of sassafras saplings in the woods. It was a tree, not very large. She would dig one up, cut off some of the aromatic sweet-smelling roots, wash them really good, and boil them to make tea. Root beer is made from sassafras roots, I just learned recently. One thing that always fascinated me about the sassafras tree, it has three different shaped leaves on every tree, a plain oval-shaped leaf, a leaf with two extension- like fingers, and one with three fingers like an oak leaf. Very peculiar, I always thought, on the same tree.

We loved sweet tea, considered the wine of the South, Pepsi, Dr. Pepper, and Coca-Colas. We did drink a lot of milk and Grandma would let us drink coffee, the way she liked it with lots of evaporated milk. Coffee at that time was considered an adult drink, but Grandma fixed it for us kids. Probably the men folks added a little extra something, but not at our house. Grandma loved to drink buttermilk, clabber, she called it. I thought it tasted nasty.

We didn't eat fancy food growing up, but we always had plenty and looking back, I realize that was the most important thing.

There were many people at that time that had nothing and our family was blessed. We always had food on the table and three meals a day, grits and fatback for breakfast, dinner at noon, and supper in the early evening. Families always gathered around the table at meal time; Daddy blessed the food and we all shared the days' events. Family meal-time was important, never once did we take our plate and sit in front of the television. It was turned off during meals. It was considered family time.

15. Grandma, Wisdom and Patience

When I think of my grandma, I think about the time period her life encompassed and how things changed so much in-between. Grandma was born in 1887, the Victorian era; there were lots of things that were just not discussed in polite society. Even though her family was very poor, they were raised in the church and believed that a woman's place was in the home, and that childbirth and sex were taboo to discuss. They may have discussed these topics with other women, but not within earshot of children.

My Grandma had never worn a bathing suit, short pants or long. She always wore dresses, and at home an apron with a bib and two large pockets. She made all of her aprons and most dresses on her old treadle machine. In these apron pockets, she would carry things that she thought she might need during the day when cooking and cleaning. There were always several pretty handkerchiefs, needle and thread, small scissors and possibly twine, and of course her change purse with a few coins inside. Not only did she make her dresses and aprons, she also made some of her undergarments. I remember she had a homemade bra. She called it an underbody. She also had a lace-up pink corset like Scarlett O'Hara was trussed up in by Mammy in *Gone with the Wind*. I don't remember her wearing it, but we thought it was a wonder with all the crossed laces and the bone stays. She must have purchased that when she was very young and "strait-laced" literally.

I remember she had several hats with long hat pins, some with pearls on the end. Her hats were kept stacked one on top of the other in a short cabinet door in the chifforobe. Underneath the door, which had a mirror on it, there were four drawers. Ever industrious, we kids would pull out the drawers to different lengths starting at the bottom to form steps. This drawer ladder allowed us to climb up and open Grandma's hat cabinet and try on her hats. We must have been quite small. I have that old chifforobe, and if I was to try and stand on the edge of even one drawer, the whole thing would turn over.

Grandma's family, the Burketts, were very poor, but gentle people. They never owned any land and very few material things. They lived in many different places and worked for a landowner, living in some little wooden house on the premises, maybe with a little garden spot included.

Growing up I remember seeing many of the small tenant houses in fields grown up with weeds and broom straw. The little house would be falling down, tin blown off the roof and porches sagging. It seemed there was always a cedar beside these tenant shacks and kudzu or other vines growing up the sides. I seldom see them at all now. This was the kind of house my Grandma's family lived in.

When I think what her life was like, I realize how frugal she was taught to live. These sharecroppers knew they had to work for someone else. They didn't farm their own plot of ground. They had to be tough to survive.

I often have thought of the time period she lived in. She was born in 1887, a long time ago. The War Between the States had ended only twenty-two years earlier. That seems like a short time ago to me. I can remember my life twenty-two years ago. Can you? Not long ago at all. Her grandfather was a Confederate soldier and most of her uncles had been in the fight. Her father was born, the youngest, in 1860.

When she was born there were still hostile Indians on the Great Plains and millions of buffalo. It was still considered the Wild West. Billy the Kid had been killed in 1881, the same year as the fight at the O.K. Corral with Doc Holiday and the Earp Brothers. This took place only six years before her birth. The Oklahoma land rush was in 1889 when Grandma was two years old. Before she passed away in November 1974, Neil Armstrong had stepped foot on the moon. Her life began in the horse and buggy days, and ended with rockets launched into space.

Grandma was a product of her birth, Victorian in thought and manners. She was Christian in her beliefs and practices. She loved all people. She never said an unkind word about any race and was always the very definition of patience. I know this because of the many times we tried her patience and she never showed any signs of anger.

I can vividly remember taking her can of talcum powder, dumping most of it on the floor in the hallway, jumping off her trunk with our socks on, and slipping and sliding in the powder.

I believe that would have pushed me over the edge, but she didn't even complain. She may have made us clean up our mess, but I don't think she did. I never recall us doing anything that flustered her.

In 1959 when Buster, "aka Steve," went to school, the first day, he refused to get on the school bus. Grandma took his arm to guide him to the bus. He was determined he was not going and slung poor Grandma around in the front yard. She was a little woman and holding onto him was like trying to hold a slippery eel. He finally got on the bus and when Daddy got home from work, Steve got what he so justly deserved. I'm not sure who squealed on him, probably one of us kids, not Grandma. Grandma was such a pushover.

Thinking back now, I believe because of her age and hard life, she was just too tired and let any aggravation we caused her slide off like "water off a duck's back." She had so much sorrow and trouble in her life, we kids gave her purpose and she paid no attention to our unruly actions. She loved us unconditionally, even spending her little monthly check of $30.00 on us.

During the summers, tinkers would come by the house selling all manner of household products: pots and pans, rugs, pictures, blankets, flavorings, powdered puddings, salves, anything and everything. Grandma would sometimes buy from these traveling salesmen; usually she knew them as a distant relative or someone that had been by before. If she bought anything, it was some medicinal salve in a tin for her aching arthritic hands. Most often it was something she wanted us to have.

In March of 1959, Grandma Florence went to the doctor and he sent her to the hospital. She went to the hospital on April 1st and stayed until April 11th. Grandma had uterine cancer. We kids did not know that at the time, but we knew she was very sick.

Of course, Daddy couldn't miss work so he had to figure out how to get us back and forth to school while he worked. I remember Aunt Fannie and Uncle Willie came and stayed with us a couple of nights, and saw that we were fed and sent to school. Then they had to go home and tend to their animals. Daddy started getting us up early, taking us to their house on the main highway so we could catch the bus. In the evenings, we would get off the bus at Aunt Jennie and Uncle Olin's. Aunt Jennie was good to us; I remember the wonderful strawberries she would give us with real cream. Uncle Olin was not mean, he just didn't say much. I thought he was just an old grouch.

Daddy would go to the hospital in Columbia to visit Grandma, while we kids waited in the car for what seemed like hours. No one ever bothered us; it was definitely a different world back then. Children were not allowed to even sit in the hospital lobby in those days, so we waited, never getting out of the car. We knew the rules.

That was a hard time for my Daddy. Aunt Bessie and Uncle Leon had both taken jobs at Lakeside Nursing Home in Lexington and helped as attendants for the old folks there. That's why they couldn't stay with us. I have no clue where our mother was or our other grandparents, Coley and Sarah Bell Hartley. I never remember them coming to see us while we lived in the old house. They may have helped with our care, but I'm sure my daddy didn't want to ask, so Uncle Willie and Aunt Fannie took charge. I do remember Aunt Fannie let me stay home from school one day because I felt bad. She always called me "Catty."

When Grandma came home, she talked about having cobalt treatments while in the hospital. She seemed to be completely well. God knew we needed her and she recovered.

16 Remembering Rayflin

All my life, Rayflin was considered the original home-place. My great Grandparents, Kel and Peninnah Woodward Gantt lived there until they passed away, Kel in 1930 and Peninnah in 1949. After their deaths, the homeplace passed to Aunt Jennie and Uncle Olin. I recall visiting there many times as a child and Aunt Jennie had cared for us when Grandma was in the hospital.

If Uncle Leon walked down to Rayflin, chances were really good that I walked with him. The house was a big farmhouse that had been expanded by five rooms in the early twentieth century. Unlike the old house where we lived, it was painted white. The house sat close to a curve in the dirt road and was only a few hundred yards from the North Edisto River. All us kids loved to visit Aunt Jennie. Her older two children were girls, Virginia and Mildred, the boys were around my daddy's age or younger, George, Gantt, and Charles.

When I visited there with Uncle Leon, he would sit on the L-shaped front porch with Uncle Olin and other male visitors, smoking, chewing tobacco, and talking. Not me, them. Near the end of their lives, I remember Uncle Rion and Uncle Sammy, my

Granddaddy Kelly's brothers, being there. I did not talk to them. I was just a little kid, but I would sit and listen as Uncle Leon talked to his old uncles. Boy, have I heard stories about them in their youth! They were both wild and big drinkers in their younger years. When I knew them they were just old. I also remember Aunt Corrie, Granddaddy Kelly's sister. Aunt Corrie lived in Atlanta, I think, with Nina Lee or Sis. Uncle Cyrus lived in Florida. I never remember seeing him.

When we kids spent time at Aunt Jennie's while Grandma was in the hospital we played in the yard around the big house. The huge magnolia tree still shadowed the front porch and another one stood beside the back porch near the kitchen, crunchy dried leaves a carpet beneath both. One thing that stands out in my memory is Aunt Jennie's flower pit behind the house. A big square hole about four feet deep with a low bench on each of the four sides on the bottom. Aunt Jennie's potted plants were kept here in the winter. I guess they were safe from freezing in this pit. Someone would have needed a ladder to place and remove the plants. We kids were leery of playing near it, afraid we would fall in. No telling what kind of creatures were hiding under those low benches.

There was also a smokehouse across from the pit. There was a large fig bush right beside the door and in the summer time it was full of figs. When we visited and the figs were ripe, we would help ourselves. Aunt Jennie didn't mind. One step up from the ground and we could open the smokehouse door. I only remember darkness and dusty shelves. Its original purpose had long been deserted. That old smokehouse still stands today, in 2018, covered with tangled vines, briars, and weeds. It would take a machete to hack a path into that old building today. Of the house itself, a burned-out shell, only part of the bedroom beside the front door to the left still stands. What is left is all overgrown, it can barely be glimpsed surrounded by a jungle. The original house with the rock chimney towards the road was completely destroyed by fire. The rock chimney stood for a number of years on its own, then finally collapsed in a heap.

I know the original house was constructed with home-made nails and wooden pegs. It was there during the War Between the States. Some of Sherman's legion built a fire next to one of the supporting pillars hoping to burn the house but did not succeed. They rode off on their horses too soon, and some of the family ran out to rake the fire out before it could spread. Great- grandmother Peninnah, was a five-year-old child then and lived there with her grandparents, Russell and Elizabeth Nelson Gunter.

The smokehouse also could have well been there when Sherman's men came through. There's no telling when it was actually built. My best guess is long, long ago. Across the road are the remains of Great-Granddaddy Kel's corn crib. Everything else has been destroyed. The barns, fenced pastures and cleared fields, all grown up now with pines. The terraces between these large plowed fields have been washed away, no longer visible or remembered by any living family member. Uncle Leon told me Granddaddy Kel had farm equipment, plows, hay rakes, stalk cutters, mule harnesses and gear, wagons, buggies, and a complete set of blacksmith tools. He said the farm was called a five-mule farm, which he indicated meant it was considered a large operation when Kel Gantt was in charge.

Back to the memories of my youth. While we stayed with

Aunt Jennie and Uncle Olin after school until Daddy got off work, they took us to Leesville to visit their son Gantt Rish's store to buy groceries. That seemed like the longest trip of my young life. Uncle Olin drove twenty miles an hour the whole way to Leesville. I know because I peeked over the seat at the speedometer. I found a little green plastic cow in the backseat and tried to amuse myself with that. I'm sure it belonged to their grandson, Randy. I remember being at Aunt Jennie's one night when George, Randy's dad, and his family were there. Steve and I played in the kitchen with Randy and his fancy tin barn and all his plastic farm animals.

I remember directly in front of their house was a fenced-in pasture and a small people gate. Uncle Olin took me with him, I believe to milk a cow. I only recall he was carrying a bucket. I had heard stories about cows hating the color red, probably had seen a bull fight with a Spanish matador on TV. Anyway, I remember taking off my plastic light brown headband and leaving it outside the gate. Uncle Olin told me that was just silly, but I wasn't taking any chances. I thought the cow might think my headband was red.

Daddy took us to Aunt Jennie's on a particular night, I think because Charles was home visiting from the Navy. I remember sitting on the floor looking at Charles' girlie magazines. No adult told me I couldn't. They were actually pretty tame, nothing like *Playboy*. At least the "ladies" did have on some clothes, skimpy though they were. The grown-ups were so busy laughing and talking, they weren't paying too much attention to the kids.

I remember Mildred was five years older than Daddy and very entertaining. She had no children. Her husband, Ed Brown, and herself may have been living there at that time. I just remember her talking about her false teeth, and how she just wanted to jerk them out of her mouth and give them a toss. I don't remember the whole story, but all the adults laughed and laughed while Mildred talked. I really liked her.

    We kids had some great times in that big farmhouse. I always enjoyed being around the older folks and listening to their conversations. We were there many times growing up and were pretty much given the run of the house. I was most fascinated with the old part that was put together with wooden pegs and the fireplace in the room next to the road. Daddy said there were circular stairs that went up to a couple of attic rooms. I never saw that. Aunt Jennie did show me two large pictures, one of her father, Kel Gantt and one of Peninnah's mother, Ara Gunter. Ara had died in 1864. I'm not sure what happened to those old pictures. Uncle Leon said they were probably thrown away. Not everybody cares about their ancestors, especially when they have no idea who or what connection they are to them. Who knows? They could be hanging in a Cracker Barrel Restaurant somewhere.

17. A Tribute to Our Daddy

My Daddy really had a hard time after Momma left, but never complained or said anything to us children about her behavior or abandoning us. She would stop by once in a while and see us, but she was busy with her new friends.

Daddy was always there to take care of us, him and Grandma. When Momma showed up on Christmas Eve when I was in the third grade, I actually remember resenting her presence. I felt like her being there distracted from our celebration. We always loved her, but even as a child, I had no illusions about our importance in her life.

Daddy took time with us. He never was one to show affection easily, but we knew we were loved. He would sometimes take out his guitar and sing and play for us. We always loved his songs and sang along. He was a bluegrass music fan and loved Bill Monroe. He would sing *The Wabash Cannonball*, *The Great Speckled Bird*, *Boil Them Cabbage Down*, lots of railroad songs, country songs by Hank Snow, also Webb Pierce, and the late great Hank Williams. We kids had our favorites and would always beg him to play the *The Little Brown Church in the Wildwoods* or "Ain't gonna need this house no longer, I'm getting ready to meet the Saints."

Daddy's musical ability came naturally from Grandma's side of the family. Uncle Eugene played the banjo, Uncle James the guitar. Daddy played both the fiddle and the guitar, even Aunt Rosalee played the piano. None of them ever had a formal music lesson or could read musical notes. They all just played by ear.

Daddy did things for us other fathers didn't have time to. He took time. Once, he made us a pair of stilts. There were wedges about two feet from the ground where we placed our feet and he had smoothed the tops so we wouldn't get splinters in our hands. We had great fun clopping about the yard on our homemade stilts.

He came home from work one night. It was winter, and we were all in the warm kitchen. Steve had found two young squirrels, born early before spring had arrived; they had fallen from their nest. Buster was always bringing home some kind of critters. What were we to do? We didn't want the little babies to die. Daddy took me and Steve up to where we were building the house and we held a spotlight so that he could build a cage with chicken wire to keep them in. We filled it with cotton and put them in the hallway on top of Grandma's sewing machine. We intended to feed them milk with an eye dropper and keep them alive. Tragically, they didn't last long. Even though they had a cage full of cotton bedding, they froze to death. The hall, in the dead of winter, was actually that cold.

I can vividly remember my daddy sitting on the floor covering shoe boxes with aluminum foil and gluing valentines on them to make our valentine box for the class party. The one with the fanciest box won a prize. Knowing my Daddy took the time to sit on the floor and make my box was prize enough for me.

We were blessed with a patient, kind father. He didn't hesitate to discipline us if we deserved it, but only then. He was so like Grandma in nature, never excitable or giving us a whipping for no reason. We had sense enough to know this. His one flaw, if it could be considered that, was his stubbornness. I believe I inherited that from him, I've been told that I am stubborn.

Daddy was always a Ford man and never would consider any other brand vehicle. The first car I remember was a 1950 grey Ford sedan. The hood had a prominent, almost point in the front middle of the hood. I'm sure the grey Ford was bought used. My daddy never had a new car. He was a product of his generation, WWII, the "Greatest Generation" as it has been called. Daddy told me before he died, while he knew Toyota and Honda were good vehicles, being made by the Japanese was their flaw. Because of the War, he always considered them the enemy.

I did actually avoid a well-deserved punishment one time. I bit Lula Mae on her side. I guess I must have been one of those children that retaliated by biting any other kid that provoked me. I don't remember why, but I know I did it. Then I hid in the corner behind the bed and flat refused to come out. Daddy didn't insist. He let me get by that one time.

Heck, brother Steve couldn't have been more than six or seven when he threw a butcher knife at our cousin, Betty. It actually stuck in the kitchen wall and quivered back and forth. Betty screamed, "You're a little Devil!"

I don't remember why he did it, but I'm sure that he got a well-earned whipping from Daddy.

18. Take your Medicine

My Daddy and Grandma were great believers in preven- tive medicine. As kids playing all summer in the sandy soil in our yard, dealing with yellow flies, sand gnats, blow flies, horse flies, and the ever-present mosquitoes, we were always getting bit or stung by some insect. There were these huge red and black striped ants, which we called "cow ants." They were easy to spot and hard to kill. When we saw them, we stayed out of their way. In the spring with flowers blooming, we had to watch out for honey bees, yellow jackets, wasps, bumble bees, and dirt daubers. We always had bruises, cuts and scrapes, bee stings, and bumps on the head. These had to be attended to.

We often in the summer developed something Grandma called carbuncles, actually boils that came from bacteria entering a cut or scrape. We were given a sulfur tablet once a day. The tablet was flat and yellow, had to be chewed, and actually tasted good. It was supposed to help prevent these painful, swollen sores we called risings. The skin would swell into a painful red area. It was like a huge pimple that had to be lanced, to drain out the pus and infection. They could be anywhere on the body. I had several at different times, especially on my legs.

Before I started school, daddy took me to the Lexington County Health Department to get my required smallpox vaccination. They would not give it to me because I had one of the sores on my leg. I remember I was so happy I couldn't get the vaccination. I skipped all the way back to the car.

When I actually started to school in first grade, me and all my fellow students that had not had their smallpox vaccine were called to the office. A nurse was there to administer the vaccine. Standing in line outside the office, I was terrified. I hated shots, like my fellow classmates. I cringed to think of a needle stuck in my arm, but had no choice except to wait my turn. It was really no big deal. The nurse cleaned my upper left arm, put some green cream on a small circular spot, and took a sharp needle and jabbed in that green stuff several times. It wasn't like a regular shot with a long needle that injected the vaccine. In a couple of days, it became a sore with a scab that formed on top. We were not allowed to touch or pick at the scab since it was really smallpox. The scab would eventually fall off and leave a round scar.

We also were taken dutifully to receive our polio vaccine given in sugar cubes. Daddy saw the announcement in our local newspaper of the time and place and took us to have the vaccine. We didn't mind the polio vaccine. We didn't have to get a shot.

He eventually started giving us a small one-a-day red vitamin pill. I had a big problem swallowing pills, Daddy didn't know. I would slip out on the porch and bury my vitamin in one of Grandma's flower pots. He found out some way that I was not taking my vitamins. I bet one of my siblings snitched. Anyway, he wasn't mad. He explained that I could put it on the back of my tongue and take a big swig of water and it would be gone. I did better after that.

Of course, burns required toothpaste or baking soda and there were always Epsom salts, which was considered a cure for most everything. Grandma believed in her Milk of Magnesia; it was in a cobalt blue bottle and good old Ex-Lax ™, which really tasted like chocolate candy. Mercurochrome, Merthiolate, and iodine were dabbed on cuts and scrapes, but stung when applied except for the Merthiolate. I would whine because of the stinging and Grandma, bless her heart, would blow on my injury to cool the burning, not knowing she was adding more germs. Geritol was advertised for iron poor blood and Doan's pills for backache. Paregoric was good for stomach aches, but at the time no one realized the opium it contained was not a good thing to be uncontrolled. All of these medicines were in the medicine cabinet Granddaddy built. There was also aspirin for headaches, Mentholatum and Vicks vapor rub, ointments to rub on our chest when we had colds. The cabinet hung high on the kitchen wall to the left beside the kitchen door.

This cabinet was originally built as a letter cabinet by Granddaddy with six little cubbies for envelopes and bills received. Credit cards were not used then, at least not at our house. Payments for bills had to be mailed or paid in person with cash or by personal check. These bills we received in our mail box were called 'dones', by the grown-ups. I wondered about that name. I guess it was because they were done waiting on what we owed. This cabinet on the wall had a back board and sides shaped like the arm of a chair. I used to imagine it as a chair on the wall. *What would it be like to sit up there high above the floor,* I often thought? Daddy added a door and painted it white; that's when it became our medicine cabinet. He also added a latch, so nosy children would stay away from the contents. These medicines could have been dangerous for little children, especially the chocolate Ex-Lax ™.

We would have probably eaten the whole box with disastrous effects.

19. Health and Hygiene

I do remember having a Health book to study in grammar school. Actually, it must have not sunk in because when I was a kid we didn't take all-over baths in the winter and I'm sure that would have been covered in any health instructions. It was too cold in that old house. The kitchen was the only warm room and it was shared by all of us. There would be no privacy, water would have to heated on the stove for the bath. It made no sense because of the circumstances. We would usually wash our feet in a foot tub in front of the wood stove or the fireplace before climbing into bed. Inside the house we were always barefoot, even in the winter. So, we needed to at least wash our feet before going to bed. I don't recall having any bedroom shoes.

We were healthy considering conditions at the time. I know we had vaccinations as babies because I still have a pink card that listed what I was vaccinated for. We even on occasion had to be admitted to the hospital. According to Uncle Leon's notes, Louise had to have her appendix removed at the hospital in Columbia the night of January 7, 1957 and was released from the hospital on January 12th. Imagine five days in the hospital for appendicitis. That would be outpatient surgery today.

We all had "sore eyes" while in grammar school. We would wake up with our eyes matted shut and Grandma would have to get a warm washcloth to loosen the crusty matter so we could open our eyes and see. I am pretty sure it's called pink eye now.

We all had rotten baby teeth, no fluoride in spring water or toothpaste. It seemed we were always having toothaches and earaches, very painful as I recall. Finally, after I reached age ten, daddy took us regularly to visit Dr. Baker, a dentist in Leesville. He charged three dollars to pull a tooth and less for fillings. The first time Daddy took me, Dr. Baker said I had ten cavities. Lula Mae had twenty-one. I imagine Louise and Steve got a similar report. We ate far too much candy and did not regularly brush our teeth. Country kids were not too concerned about proper hygiene as preventive health, unless a tooth or ear started hurting. Bathing was also pretty much optional. Most all our classmates in grammar school were in the same situation and thought nothing of being stinky and dirty. I can imagine during the spring it was bad to have to teach a class of sweaty, stinky children, but we were cleaner in the summer and even got our hair shampooed.

Uncle Leon's little notebook records other health matters. We all had mumps and chicken pox. He states that, "Louise and Kathy had mumps the week of May 15th 1960. Steve had them the week before Louise and Kathy, then Lula Mae had mumps the last week in May 1960." Like most childhood diseases we passed them from one to another.

20. Changing Seasons

I don't believe the grown-ups in our house realized that we kids noticed the changes in the seasons. I know I did. There were sights, sounds, and smells that to this day remind me of memories from my childhood.

There was always the smell of chalk and the click of the brightly colored abacus beads sliding on their heavy wire. Miss Garvin tried to teach us how to count and write our letters. It was Fall. The first month of school still felt warm; some boys in grammar school even came to school barefoot. Boys and girls at my school could not to wear shorts, but I guess shoes were not a wardrobe requirement. These few kids probably were barefoot because they had no shoes to wear.

Early October, a chill filled the air and Daddy would build a small fire in the wood heater. Breezes became more noticeable and cooler. Of course, leaves begin to turn to flaming colors of red, yellow, and orange, and began to float down from the trees. Sometimes when we were on the playground a small whirlwind of sand and leaves would develop. If it moved in our direction, we closed our eyes, turned our heads from the gritty sand, and leaves tossed about until it passed. Grammar school included the first through sixth grades. But, when we advanced to fourth grade we moved upstairs and had a different playground. The slide was much higher, the swings seemed to reach to the sky, and we had a fabulous merry-go-round. The 1st, 2nd, and 3rd graders we considered babies and their playground was much tamer. We now considered ourselves upper classman, no longer little kids. We did not play together at recess. I'm sure it was solely for safety purposes because older kids can be tough and take advantage of younger naïve little kids.

I remember when I was in first grade, a couple of older girls tried to swindle me out of my spending money at recess, money Uncle Leon gave to me. Their ploy was the promise of saving our money for a party. I was a little naïve kid and they did extort my nickels and quarters a couple of times. Then I wised up. I refused to turn over my change to them. They left me alone after that, big bullies. I guess they thought I might squeal to one of my teachers. Mrs. Garvin would have had them for lunch. I was afraid of her, even though she was my teacher. That was my only experience with bullies and blackmailers. That was in first grade. When we moved upstairs, we considered ourselves grown up.

I paid close attention to the goldenrod when it began to bloom along the banks of the road. When I see their yellow blooms, I recall the first verse of a poem we read at school, in fifth grade.

The goldenrod is yellow
The corn is turning brown
The trees in apple orchards
With fruit are hanging down

All fields were overgrown with weeds and broom straw in late September and October. There was rabbit tobacco; sour grass, which we liked to chew on; little purple wild flowers; and yellow petaled flowers on slim stakes full of leaves, that we called cow weeds. Supposedly if cows ate these weeds it would sour their milk, at least that's what Grandma told us.

There were always fallen leaves that had to be raked into piles in our yard. The smell of burning leaves was ever-present in the fall, a very common smell at the end of October and into November. We didn't have grass in our yard during my childhood. Only sand, and grandma's plants, but the yard had to be raked. That seemed to be the rule at all homes of country folks. There was something important about having a raked yard, even if it was only sand.

We also picked up all the green balls under the big Black Walnut tree near the road and piled them on the ground beside the car-shed. Eventually the green, spongy outside would rot away and leave a pile of walnuts, which Grandma would crack with a hammer. Black Walnuts were hard nuts to crack. The meat of the nuts was picked out by Grandma and used in baking. Of course, we ate them too.

Another memory of fall to me was the cutting of wood by Daddy and Uncle Leon. Their saw had a huge vertical round blade with sharp teeth, and sat on a trailer with two wheels and a motor. They towed the saw out of the tin car-shed with brute force to the woodpile. It had a gasoline motor. The blade would spin when one of them yanked the rope to crank it, much like grass mowers that have to be pushed. If I concentrate, I can still hear the whine of that saw as Uncle Leon and Daddy stood on either side, wearing heavy leather gloves as they pushed wood through the saw. One of them would then toss the wood on a pile with a resounding plop and I could hear a hum as they communicated with each other above the din of the whirling blade. They did this late in the evenings in October and November preparing for winter because we had to keep a good supply of wood for the heater in our kitchen and the fireplaces.

There were a lot of sawmills in the area and slabs would be given away to anyone willing to haul them off. They cut a lot of pine slabs, which are the outer portion of the pine trunk with the bark still on it. They also cut hardwood, but that involved cutting down the tree or cutting up limbs that had fallen from trees in the woods during a windy thunder storm. Green wood, that lasts longer in the fire had to come from living trees. Dry wood burned much faster and was mostly pine wood that had been cut a while, long enough to dry. They would cut hardwoods by using an axe to chop a triangle gash in the side of the tree, then, when it was halfway through, push it over from the opposite side. Of course, they had to be sure we children were not around.

When a hurricane comes through, I think of Hurricane Hazel. Hurricane Hazel came ashore in the morning of October 15, 1954, per Uncle Leon's notes. I'm sure we were forewarned by newspaper and radio but had no idea of the devastation a strong storm could cause. The only reason, I remember at age three, was the fact a huge tree was blown over down by the spring at the swamp's edge, with a mass of root-filled dirt at one end of the trunk and the huge tree blown over like it was swatted by a giant hand. I remember climbing on the downed tree and playing among the limbs. Uncle Leon and my daddy used axes and a crosscut saw to remove the limbs.

Winter was around the corner when all the trees were bare of their foliage.

The mornings were chilly, and Daddy had to keep the fire going with a bed of coals through the night. Then the next morning he added some fat lighter, pieces of dry wood and some green wood. By the time we hopped out of bed, there would be a nice warm fire waiting in the kitchen stove.

The sight of smoke trailing away from the kitchen chimney and the smell of the wood burning were the first changes that meant winter was upon us.

The one thing we kids were expected to do was carry wood to the boxes on both porches. Our job was to keep them full. This was an evening job, one we did before it got dark. Sometimes, Grandma would take an axe and a croker sack and go into the woods across the road. She was in search of pine tree stumps to cut splinters from the heart of the stump. It was called "fat lighter." The splinters had a distinct pine smell, rich with sap and orange in color. I would still recognize that smell today, close to pine sol cleaner.

Some of us kids were always along with Grandma when she went in search of splinters as fire starter. She would use the axe to cut small splinters from the old pine stumps. Thinking back an axe should have been replaced by a hatchet, maybe that's why we went with her, simply to make sure she returned safely. She could have swung the long-handled axe and hit herself, after all she was well in her seventies and a very small person. When the sack was half full, we would carry it back. The splinters were emptied into a separate small wood box in the kitchen.

An electric light was turned on in the pump house and the outside spigot was wrapped to keep it from freezing up. We also had to fill the water buckets every evening. When we filled the buckets, we frequently spun round and round holding the full bucket by the handle. The water, of course, did not spill while we were spinning due to centrifugal force, just like when an automatic washer goes through a spin cycle and the clothes are plastered to the sides of the tub. That was fun for us.

With the cold of winter, we didn't stand outside on the porch waiting for the bus. We kept watch from the windows by the door, with our coats on and books in a stack within easy reach. I don't remember having a book bag. Sometimes boys would cinch their books together with a belt and sling it over their shoulder. Girls never did that.

If it got below freezing there would be crystals of ice that spewed up in damp places beside the road. Any puddles left from a rain would have a skimming of ice on top. No matter how cold, girls had to wear dresses or skirts and blouses to school, no long pants were allowed. That was the dress code the whole time I was in school.

***

Of course, in the winter at home, we still were allowed outside to play, we just had to bundle up. The only time we had to stay in was pouring rain. When rain came down in sheets and the temperature was not too cold, we played on the North porch. Sometimes we splashed in the water coming off the roof, sticking our hands in the curtain pouring from above or we splashed each other, anything to entertain. That was our goal. Steve had a red metal fire truck, probably a gift from Santa on Christmas. It was wonderful fun, pushing each other the length of the porch in Steve's fire truck. It had small wooden ladders attached to the sides, peddles to propel the rider, steering wheel, and even a bell attached to the top of the hood. Being kids, we would lift our feet, ignoring the peddles, and push the occupant as fast as possible from one end of the porch to the other.

The wind would blow and seep in around the windows. Often at night we would hear owls hoot down near the spring, foxes yelp outside, or dogs barking in the distance. Our dogs barked, too, if anyone or anything strange was happening in the woods. I hated hearing barking dogs; it frightened me. Our dogs lived outside, even in the winter. They always had the porches to sleep on or they slept under the smokehouse or car-shed. We never worried about them since they had a thick coat of fur in the winter and were well fed.

On winter days we played behind the tin car-shed. The sun reflecting off the tin created a warm space. We would carry our toys, mostly our dolls, and sit against the warm tin. Even on a cold day, if it was sunny and the wind wasn't blowing it was a great place to play.

***

I noticed the small green shoots beginning to burst forth on the scrub oaks beside the playground at school. Spring had arrived. We played in those woods every day at recess. Games children played when they had to have imagination. It was mostly hide-and-seek in the woods for the girls.

We watched so many westerns on TV back then, the boys, of course, loved to play cowboys and Indians. It wasn't against the rules to bring your holster and silver metal six shooters to school. This was during the cold war, so we were all schooled about bomb shelters and what to do in case those evil Russians should attack. We were told to duck under our desks. So, in the context of the time, war was also a popular game for the boys. Ducking and weaving through the trees, hiding behind bushes, they would yell, "Surrender or I'll shoot! Drop your weapon now!" Of course, as a general rule, their weapon was a thumb with an index finger as the barrel.

On the big kids' playground, sun beamed brightly and soft breezes were blowing. Not too hot or cold, we would take off our jackets, slide down the big slide, or swing as high as we could then jump out when the swing reached its apex. Surprisingly, children could do things like that and land hands in the sand on all fours, jump up, and start all over. There was also a merry-go-round which everyone loved. We had to push it ourselves and then jump on.

Children were always running, especially when spring was in the air. I remember the smell of yellow jasmine and honeysuckle in the spindly oaks beside the sandy playground. The air smelled sweet.

Boys and girls played games together: Red Rover, tug of war

with a rope, and red-light-green-light. I don't even remember how the latter was played, sort of like Simeon Says, I think. We all, boys and girls, liked to play "drop the handkerchief." We also played catch a lot, chasing each other all over the sandy playground. There was not a blade of grass on either playground when I attended grammar school. If you saw grass, don't be fooled, it was only sandspurs. The school yard had a lot of those. That was probably why the school newspaper in high school was called the "Sandspur." I hated sandspurs and beggar lice, another plant that returned in spring, with little black flat seeds that clinged to our clothes. The beggar lice had to be removed individually, no brushing those suckers off. Be assured all this play was supervised by watchful teachers and our principal, Mr. Nichols. They would make sure we were behaving. Sometimes I think if we could go back to the '50s it would be a good thing.

I loved spring at our house, too. The yard was almost all sand, no grass. Somehow grandma could make flowers grow in that sandy soil. When her rose bush at the end of the house bloomed, it smelled so sweet. She had angel trumpets, spider lilies, gladiolas, irises, hibiscus, and daffodils. Both my sisters love flowers like Grandma. I was never much of a gardener.

***

Easter was soon upon us. We always had to have at least three or four dozen boiled eggs. We would drop a colored tablet in each cup, then add vinegar and hot water. I would still recognize the special smell of that egg dye. We each had a cup and would drop a boiled egg in it and keep turning it over so the color would be even. There were little copper wire dippers to turn the egg and take it out of the cup when it was colored. The egg dying was always done one night after supper, on newspaper spread on the kitchen table. Grandma didn't want egg dye on her table cloth. When all the eggs were dyed, we would put them in a basket or big bowl to admire our handiwork. The cups of leftover dye, we took outside and poured them on poor Susie, one of our three dogs that followed us everywhere. Her fur was completely white and we thought we were just making her look "Easterly." She really didn't seem to mind and the dye soon washed off in the first spring rain.

After church and dinner on Easter Sunday, we immediately started the egg hunts. Daddy and Uncle Leon would hide the eggs and we would find them. After they got tired of hiding eggs, we kids would take turns, each hid them and the other three would hunt for them. We would do this for several days. Any eggs we lost, the dogs would eventually find and eat. We didn't leave a basket out for the Easter Bunny to fill, but would usually receive a solid chocolate bunny, some jelly beans, or the large marshmallow-filled candy eggs in different colors. One year, I remember, we received a paper mache bunny with a backpack filled with jelly beans, nestled on shiny green fake grass.

***

We looked forward to May 1st, the day Grandma let us take off our shoes and go barefoot. What I really reminisce most about spring, sitting on the high end of our porch and hearing the rain coming across the cornfield. It smelled so nice after a spring rain and at night the sound of rain hitting the tin roof would lull me off to sleep. It was still comfortable in our bedroom before the sultry summer arrived. We didn't need cover or a fan to keep us cool.

Many nights in the spring, the men folks; Uncle Leon, Daddy, and Grandma's brothers Willie, Eugene, Bunyan, and James; would sit on the front porch and talk. They would have the porch light off and the hall light would shine through the screen door. The porch light was off so the bugs and flying insects were not as bothersome. I think this was my most favorite season. They would talk, smoke, or chew tobacco and we kids would play in the front yard. "There ain't no booger man out tonight" was our favorite game. One of us would hide at the edge of the yard and the others would march down the brick-lined front walk singing. "There ain't no booger man our tonight 'cause Papa killed them all." It was dark and we were waiting for the booger man to jump out and scare us, then we would race back to the porch.

Across the road we could see lightning bugs and hear chuck-wills-widow or their cousins, whippoorwills. Sometimes other night birds like owls or nocturnal small animals would appear, flying squirrels gliding from tree to tree or even bats. The stars seemed brighter, and the moon, too, for some reason. The air smelled sweet because of Grandma's flowers and the wild flowering vines of yellow jasmine and honeysuckle in the woods. It was a great time and place to be a kid.

***

When school finally ended for the year, we were outside all day long roaming the woods. We looked for gooseberries to pick and Grandma would bake a pie if we brought enough home, after eating our fill. We had been taught what berries we could eat and which were poisonous. We ate muscadines – we called them bullises, scuppernongs, sparkle berries, blackberries, and something we called rabbit apples. They grew on a spindly little tree with huge slender thorns. There was always lots of plum trees that bordered the big cornfield. The sand was so hot we would run to the lone pine in the center of the field and stand in its shade to cool our burning feet, then make a dash to the plum trees at the edge of field to pick the plums. We knew what we could and couldn't eat. We recognized poison sumac, poison oak, and poison ivy. That didn't, however, mean we were immune. I have had my share of pink calamine lotion spread on a horrible case of poison oak that I don't even want to recall.

***

One summer Uncle Leon made us the greatest outdoor shower. He poured a cement pad behind the pump house. When it had set-up enough, he built a frame around the pad about four-by-four feet in size, put a brace across the top, and covered the whole frame in tin. There was a tin door which had a screen latch on the outside and one on the inside. Because it was just a frame there were plenty of places to put out soap, shampoo and wash cloths. The braces between the two-by-fours of the frame made great shelves. We hung our towels over the door and back wall to keep them dry until we needed them. All we had to do was hook up the water hose and throw it across the brace on top. Of course, it had to be a hot day because the water from the hose was cold. But it was wonderful in the breathless, muggy months of July and August. We all thought Uncle Leon was a genius. He was a really smart man.

The night time in July and August were especially uncomfortable to sleep. We did not even have an electric fan. We lay on the bed and fanned ourselves with a folded newspaper or a cardboard church fan until we fell asleep. We would wake up during the night drenched in sweat and fan some more until we went back to sleep. All the windows were up, with only a screen between us and the darkness of night. Sometimes, especially if it was raining, it was cool enough to sleep. Otherwise the cover was turned back and I lay on the bed in my baby doll pajamas.

21. Special People I Loved

Two people that I loved very much and were important to us as children were Aunt Elsie and Uncle Fred Ridgell. Aunt Elsie was daddy's half-sister and they were very close. They came to visit us often and always bought clothes for us. They had one son, Tony. He was a lot older than us, but was kind.

Tony and his wife, Peggy, thought about his little ragamuffin cousins at Christmas. Tony is about sixteen years older than I am. He's past eighty years old and doesn't look it. He said they would always visit Granddaddy Kelly at the old house every Sunday when he was a child. That was before Steve and I were born. I've always thought Tony looked more like his Gantt relatives than the Ridgells.

Aunt Elsie and Uncle Fred lived in a nice house on East Liberty Street in Batesburg. Visiting them, when I was a child, I can remember Aunt Elsie always had a spotless house. Sitting in their small den, I could see under their bed in the next room. Even then I thought, *it's so clean and dust free, I bet a person could eat off the floor under that bed.* Our house was never that spotless. If there was something we wanted to stash out of site, under the bed it would go, not at Aunt Elsie's. All the floors were clean, no dust on the furniture and waxed to a shiny finish.

Uncle Fred loved to fish and he loved to talk. I think he would embarrass Aunt Elsie. She was always shy and reserved, a private and very proper lady. Uncle Fred would strike up a conversation with anyone. Daddy remarried when I was almost twelve years old to Jeanette Gunter. We had already moved in the new house. Daddy said when he and Momma Jeanette went with Fred and Elsie on vacation, Fred would often talk to people in the next car at stop lights. He would roll down the window and strike up a conversation. Before the light changed, he knew where the strangers were from and their names. He was just that kind of person.

I remember spending the weekend with Aunt Elsie and Uncle Fred sometimes. Their house was always spotless and I liked sleeping in Tony's old room. The furniture was antique and polished. The wooden floors so shiny, I could see my reflection.

Uncle Fred was the first person to take me to a real restaurant for lunch. We went to a café on the corner of Oak Street in Batesburg. I had never ordered at a restaurant. I must have been eleven or twelve years old, maybe younger. I don't remember what I ordered. I do remember my lunch included a salad, which the waitress brought to me first.

Uncle Fred said, "Aren't you going to go ahead and eat your salad?"

I remember replying, "No, I will wait until I get my other food."

He kinda laughed but didn't say anything. I didn't know then that usually the salad is served first and eaten before the main entrée. He knew I was just a silly little country kid.

Once at Thanksgiving, I went with Uncle Fred to a turkey farm somewhere near Batesburg. I remember there were lots of turkeys, all with white feathers. Uncle Fred picked out one; the farmer caught it and took it away to kill. I didn't see that part. Uncle Fred paid for the turkey and placed it on newspaper in the trunk of their two-toned, black and white 1955 Chevrolet. We drove to the house of a black lady and gave her the turkey to clean and dress for Thanksgiving. I don't remember if she was going to cook the turkey, too.

Uncle Fred loved to fish, and was a collector of the most beautiful carnival glass and dispensary bottles. For those who have never heard of the dispensary system, it was a state-run monopoly in South Carolina on the sale of liquor. This system existed from 1893 until 1907 and only liquor sold in these bottles and through the state system were legal.

He always would remind Aunt Elsie about the time he found a dispensary bottle with a real paper label and she washed the label off. Every time he brought that story up, she would say, "Just hush, Fred." He loved to tease her about that because, of course, the bottle would have been much more valuable with the label on.

Aunt Elsie and Uncle Fred frequently bought clothes for us, not just at Christmas. They bought us long footy pajamas one winter, matching shorts and shirts in the summer, baby doll pajamas for summer, and long pants and shirts to match for Christmas. The first pair of shorts I ever owned probably came from Aunt Elsie. Most of the time in the summer we girls wore dresses, but not our best, of course.

***

When Grandma Florence passed away in November 1974, Aunt Elsie wanted to buy her burial clothes. She bought her a pretty pink gown and robe, far fancier than anything Grandma had ever owned. But she wouldn't have worn it anyway. She always saved anything fancy, didn't want to wear it for every day. The last couple years of her life she spent a lot of time in bed, so it was appropriate how she was dressed. In those last years, Grandma had an electric blanket. Weighing less than ninety pounds, that was the most wonderful thing ever invented, in her eyes.

I do know Aunt Elsie loved my Daddy. She and Uncle Leon were much older than he. I have pictures of Daddy as a baby. He was such a cute little boy, with blue eyes like Granddaddy Kelly and Grandma Florence.

Aunt Elsie and Uncle Leon always called Grandma, Miss Florence. They were both always kind to her and considered Robert was their brother, not only a half-brother. They both loved my daddy and us kids and of course we loved them. They were good to us; so was Uncle Fred.

22. Aunt Fannie and the Cats

*Sometime in the late '50s Aunt Fannie brought us an unex-*pected gift. She arrived with a croker sack tied shut with a thick piece of twine. We kids immediately noticed the burlap bag was moving, snarling and meowing. Aunt Fannie had somehow managed to trap three feral cats in her barn across the highway from the house where she and Uncle Willie lived. As soon as she loosened the twine around the bag, cats seemed to scatter in all directions, under the smokehouse, under the house, and one up the chinaberry tree. They were about half grown, very wild and all female tabbies. Only one had some yellow mixed along her back. We immediately named them Martha, Mary, and Susie. Now we kids had a real mission: tame these wild cats.

There was a hole already cut in the bottom of the door of the smokehouse just big enough for the cats to enter and we decided to start working on them inside the dark, dusty smokehouse. We would take table scraps in a tin plate and a dish of water to the little house with Leon written in white paint on the door. Then we would lure the cats with, "Here kitty, kitty." Eventually they got hungry and started to sneak out of hiding to eat the food we had concealed in the dark little building. At first, we didn't attempt to approach them. We wanted them to become familiar with their new home and the fact that we brought them food.

Uncle Leon or Daddy built a platform at the edge of the backyard beside our climbing tree. The platform was about three feet high and had a pole leading to an opening at the top. The scraps could be raked onto the platform and the cats could climb up to eat their food unmolested by our three dogs. We fed the dogs on a cast iron tray on the ground below. The tray was originally the base that a small wood stove rested on.

Once the cats became used to our presence, they would fly to the platform, climb the pole knowing food would be waiting. We kids could then pet them while they were busy eating. We knew we had to be smart to tame three wild cats. After they got used to our rubbing their backs while eating, they would come out of hiding and hang around when we were in the backyard. Martha especially became a sweet cat and would come whenever we called. She loved to be petted. Susie, the yellow tabby, also became completely domesticated, but Mary always was suspicious of us kids. She came when we brought food and tolerated the petting while she was eating, but otherwise she would stare at us with fright every time we came near.

It wasn't long before we realized all three were expecting kittens. There was definitely a tom cat sneaking around or when Aunt Fannie brought them they were already in the family way. We could tell their babies had been suckling and knew they were hidden away somewhere. Now all we had to do was watch them closely and when they left the yard stealthily follow at a distance hoping they would not detect that we were watching.

We found Martha's kittens, two tabbies, one completely yellow and the other grey, across the road. There were some limbs that had fallen and subsequently been covered with pine straw. Underneath the pine straw the covered limbs created a sort of tunnel system unnoticeable to the human eye. That's where Martha had hidden her two kittens. We would cross the road and sit and pet Martha and her babies, now named Dina and Cricket. They quickly became used to our attention and would come out of hiding when we kneeled on the straw-covered ground and called them.

One afternoon when we came home from school, we saw two big red hound dogs across the road sniffing among the fallen tree limbs where Martha's kittens were hidden. We were so frightened that the hounds would harm the kittens, but not enough to go to their rescue. Those red hounds were big and ferocious and we were afraid of them. When they finally left, we crossed the road and were devastated to find Dina, the yellow tabby, lying on the straw dead, killed by the dogs. As you can imagine we were inconsolable, but there was no sign of Cricket or their mother, Martha. When daddy got home from work, we couldn't wait to tell him what had happened.

"Where were the kittens hidden?" Daddy asked.

He walked across the road with all us children in tow to where poor little Dina still lay. Daddy picked up a small twig and started lifting the pine straw off the limbs, Cricket poked his head out. We were all so happy that Cricket had survived. Once again Daddy was our hero. We then buried Dina where she lay with the appropriate funeral rites accorded by young children. I'm sure we also added a bunch of wild flowers on top of her grave.

Cricket went back to the house with us. Martha didn't seem to mind sharing her baby; she was after all a loving cat and seemed to prefer our company more than her two wilder sisters. Cricket spent a lot of time indoors after that. Grandma Florence allowed him access, but not all of the time. I do remember after Cricket was older and weaned from his mother, his being inside in the winter and popping his tail on the side of the red hot wood stove. Boy did the smell of burning cat hair stink. He must have felt the heat too, because he never did that again.

We eventually located Susie and Mary's kittens and worked on taming them. Susie had her babies in the strangest place of all. She had them in the middle of the chinaberry tree next to the spigot. The two chinaberry trees were huge in circumference, with gigantic roots above the ground and big limbs that spread in every direction. The kittens were tucked away in the spot where the limbs spread out from the trunk, on a soft bed of yellow chinaberry leaves. This intersection was only six or eight feet above our heads. Even though most cats wouldn't give birth in a tree, it was the ideal spot, close to the house for safety from dogs and hidden from nosey children. We would have never even suspected until we called the cats to their platform to eat and noticed Susie jumping from the chinaberry tree. That's when we found her babies. We finally found Mary's after trying many times to follow her when she left the yard. They were found hidden, I think, in a tangle of vines and briars not far from the house. They came out when their mother meowed and we nabbed them. At first they hissed at us, but we held them, spoke softly and petted them. Soon they were tamed too.

23. Our Climbing Tree

Between the cat food platform and the plowed rows of the north field was a favorite tree we climbed. It became our "Climbing Tree." The path to the outhouse was between the feeding platform and our tree. I'm not sure what kind of tree it actually was. The grownups called it a hedge tree, which may have referred more to its location then its scientific name.

The bark as I remember was smooth and gray, the trunk about twelve inches in diameter and it had lots of branches with small green leaves. The lowest limbs we could jump up and grab, throw our leg over and pull ourselves up. It was easy to climb. There were four main limbs, two in the middle close to the trunk and two that were longer and went in the other directions; we therefore each had our own limb to claim. Steve and I, being the youngest, staked claim to the center limbs. Mine was the best. It had three smaller limbs close together, bowed outward like a chair bottom. It was pretty comfortable to just sit on. Of course, we could climb higher above on our large limb, but usually took toys and sat on our special spot. It was fun to be above the ground, tell jokes and talk. The dogs couldn't reach us, but sometimes we would bring Martha or one of the other six kittens we had. They were at home in our tree house. We took some boards and propped across some of the limbs for more space.

Then Louise, the oldest, discovered the joy of reading. She insisted that we be quiet while she read Robert Lewis Stevenson's epic, *Treasure Island*. As you can imagine, Steve and I, being six and eight had not really gotten into reading and preferred to play some other game. Louise was a real taskmaster and insisted we be quiet and listen, so we tried. Now whenever we all climbed our special tree, we could expect a reading by older sister, Louise. It did kinda grow on us, if we could pay attention. She never finished reading the whole book to us and I have never finished it.

***

Steve and I returned to more entertaining games, sometimes with Lula Mae and Louise, and sometimes just me and him. Steve had some little cars, so we would push evaporated milk cans in the sandy soil in the backyard to make roads for his cars. We had to find ways to entertain ourselves and we did.

We built a fort once when there was a good supply of green wood on the woodpile by stacking it up, leaving a spacious area inside the walls. In the summer when there was no wood in the wood boxes, we would carry our dolls and what we called supplies, climb in the empty wood box and pretend we were in the middle of the ocean on a raft and could not escape. Of course, we were besieged by sharks and all manner of sea creatures. Imagination is a wonderful thing when you have it, and when my siblings and I were growing up imagination was the key to our entertainment. There was nothing on the television in the afternoons except soap operas or game shows like *To Tell the Truth*, *Queen for a Day*, or *Concentration*, nothing we were interested in. We stayed outdoors where our pets became our companions, the woods and fields our playground, and thought of fun things to do.

The driveway was sloped downward. We would lie down on the ground at the top and roll over and over until we got to the bottom. We also would hold our arms straight out, turn around and round until we were so dizzy, we would fall down. Believe me, that was great fun for six- and eight-year-olds. Sometimes we would put a blindfold on one of the others and lead them around, giving the blindfolded one directions on where to step and what obstacles were in their way. We didn't always give truthful directions.

"Take a really big step, there's a pile of dog mess right in front of your left foot, or step over the ditch," one of our leaders would say. Of course, they knew full well the blindfolded one would step right in it and would probably fall down in the ditch. Snatching off the blindfold they had to hop to the backyard spigot to remove the offending substance that had squished up between their toes. Pulling these little pranks on each other were soon forgiven, after a "just wait until it's your turn to be led around, I'll get you both back." That was entertainment.

Sometimes we even played the blind-fold game inside, usually in the living room, when we had young visitors. Aunt Rosalee and Uncle Lewis would sometimes visit and with eleven children, nine boys, some were definitely in our age range. Uncle Lewis was a farmer and once planted Uncle Leon's fields. His boys helped with the planting while Aunt Rosalee visited with her sister, Florence. Grandma was the oldest and Aunt Rosalee her baby sister, twenty-five years younger. If it started to rain, which I recall happening, during the planting, the boys took a break and came inside. That's when we played Blind-Man's Bluff in the house. There were rules: one person was blindfolded, the game was confined to one room, and the object was to be so quiet that the blindfolded one walking around with extended hands could not locate you. If they did touch someone, then they had to guess who they had snagged. If they guessed correctly, then they were "it."

24. The Local Country Store

The nearest town with a real grocery store was fifteen miles from where we lived, but there were nearer alternatives when it came to necessities.

Steadman; only two miles away over a dirt, bumpy, washboard road full of potholes; had a country store we frequented. Mr. Cliff Rish ran the store and had canned goods, glass jars filled with cookies, and shelves with loaves of sliced bread. I remember the one with the little blonde headed girl wearing a blue dress, Sunbeam Bread, I think. Anyway, Daddy would stop there when we needed something and Steadman was where we attended church so he knew most of the folks.

But the best, bar none, country store was Gantt Brothers out on the highway near Black Creek. It was run by Danel (Daniel) and Woodrow Gantt, my Granddaddy Kelly's first cousins. Daniel and Woodrow were sons of Uncle Babe Gantt, but both were more Uncle Leon's age than my Granddaddy Kelly's. I remember going to their store many times as a child and believe me when I say, if they didn't have it in stock, you didn't need it. I enjoyed all my trips to their store. Woodrow was the most entertaining of the two, Daniel seemed to be easier going, but they both loved to talk.

They had the store full of almost anything you can imagine: shoes, clothes, mechanical tools, car parts, medicine, canned goods, buckets, yard rakes, hoes, brooms, large drink box with cold drinks, and all manner of goodies for kids. The floor was wood and slightly uneven, and there were shelves on both side walls and a counter with a glass case on the left with an adding machine, which was where Daniel was most of the time, behind the counter. The glass case held all the candy, except chocolate candy. The chocolate candy was kept in a refrigerator that stood in the middle of the room. In the summertime it kept the chocolate from melting. There was no air conditioning.

While Daniel waited on customers, Woodrow, the more talkative of the brothers, entertained with conversation. Woodrow was a talker, no doubt, and the customers enjoyed his opinions freely shared. At the end of the desk was a large meat cooler for sausage and meats of all kind. There was a woodstove for heat in the winter time that kept the store at a tolerable temperature, at least near the front counter.

One Saturday I went with Daddy out to Gantts Store. I don't remember why it was just Daddy and me, but as soon as we got out of the car it began to rain and we made a dash for the covered dirt area in the front of the store. There was a step up and double doors with double screen doors in front. Colonial Bread was written in yellow fancy script across both screens. As soon as we got inside it started pouring rain, thunder and lighting, a terrific thunder storm was breaking all around us. The rain came down in solid sheets and didn't appear to be letting up. Daddy decided we should just wait out the storm, he talking to Danel and Woodrow while I sat listening. The thing I remember most was Daddy bought me all kind of goodies while we were there, chocolate milk, Yoo Hooes of course in glass bottles, candy, and gigantic cookies from the Lance jar. That's what I remember most and the fact that I had Daddy all to myself, which was unusual.

One night I went to Gantts Store with Daddy and Uncle Leon because they needed haircuts and Woodrow was a barber. We walked over to an old unpainted house behind a rail fence in a field. It was to the left of the store about one hundred yards. Woodrow opened the door and turned on the light. In a room to the left was a fancy red barber chair. That was the first barber chair I ever saw. Woodrow cut Daddy and Uncle Leon's hair, and I just sat and listened to them talk. I was a little kid and they paid me no mind.

I never heard from anyone where the old house building came from. I do remember Danel and his wife, Kitty, lived in an apartment in the back of the store. Woodrow and his wife, Juanita, lived in a block house past the old barber shop toward Fairview with their two daughters, Deborah and Nancy. We rode the bus with them for many years.

***

At Fairview crossroads, Mr. Cleve Padgett also ran a store. It was the one we most often visited. I remember, as a child, we loved to go to Mr. Cleve's. He was a tall, big man with white hair and a mustache; he wore glasses and smoked cigars. He and his wife, Miss Maybelle, lived right next door to the store. When Daddy took us to Mr. Cleve's we bought mostly just what we needed plus a few extras we could talk Daddy into buying, like candy, cookies, or gum.

Daddy would buy us penny candies; they were located in the middle of the store in a glass case. Sometimes two pieces could be purchased for a penny, so a dime's worth of penny candy was a small paper bag full. We loved Squirrel nuts, Atomic Fireballs, Mary Janes, and those candies with caramel wrapped around a center of white cream. They were my favorites. There were also Kits taffy, four pieces wrapped together, in different flavors, and of course, Tootsie Rolls, and those little drink bottle shaped wax candies with liquid in the middle. Just bite off the top and drink the sweet liquid inside. Children could also buy candy cigarettes. They came in what looked like a cigarette box, full of some kind of mint tasting white sticks, even red coloring on the tip to give the impression of fire on the end. We kids liked to pretend we were smoking, but we didn't care for the mint taste. I did love Tootsie Roll Pops and Sugar Daddies. Both came on a white cardboard stick. Sugar Daddies were the best, but they were hard as a rock, we couldn't bite them without chipping a tooth and it took a long time to lick them. They were kinda like an all-day sucker, they lasted a long time. Also popular when I was a kid were animal crackers in a red box with a circus train on the side and a string handle. It was always fun to eat Cracker Jacks, popcorn with caramel drizzled over it, and a picture of a sailor on the side. We kids were more interested in the prize in the bottom. Sometimes we just dumped the popcorn out to get the prize. Talk about targeting the childhood audience with advertisement. Anything, cereal, or Cracker Jacks, a prize inside guarantees kids will want it. Think of market placement at cash registers, that's where most candy, gum, and packs of collectible cards are displayed. The same technique was used in most local country stores too. The drink box near the front of the store, huge glass jars of Lance cookies prominent on the counter, and candy near the check-out. Make it blatantly visible and the kiddies would insist they needed it.

I don't remember a pickle barrel, but there was a gallon jar of pickles on the counter and they were sold separately, each placed in a white, thin pickle-sized bag. There were a few chairs and a bench; it was a great place for country folks to socialize. I don't remember if beer was sold there, if it was it did not have a pull tab, you had to have a sharp punch, the kind still used to open evaporated milk cans. In the back of the store was the meat case and cheese cooler. If you wanted, Mr. Cleve would take out a long, thick stick of bologna, cut off the amount you wanted, weigh, and wrap in white butcher paper, same process with luncheon meat or hoop cheese. The cheese had a thick red wax coating and was wheel shaped. All cold drinks came in bottles. Our all-time favorite from the country store was of course an RC Cola and a Moon Pie.

25. Third Grade Was the Best

Miss Maude Shumpert taught third grade at Pelion Grammar School and before our class got there, her reputation had preceded her. She was a great teacher and we would get to do fun things in her class.

She was a nice lady, black hair and glasses. Her hair always looked exactly the same, parted on the left with a little curl on the ends. It didn't even look like she had moved a hair, so there was a rumor that she wore a wig. I don't know if that was a fact, but she never had a bad hair day. She had a great disposition and was nice to us kids. We had parties for most holidays.

First thing every morning we stood and with our hand over our hearts repeated the Pledge of Alliance to the American Flag and had prayer. Then sliding into our desk, Mrs. Shumpert would tell us, "Children take out your history book" or whatever book for the subject we were going to study.

In third grade we were taught South Carolina history. First, we started with the Indian Tribes that lived in South Carolina.

I remember the Catawba, Creek, and Pee Dee. That's when we had the teepee set up in the classroom. It was made out of heavy canvas, probably more the type used by plains Indians, not those who lived in South Carolina. We were eight-years old, we didn't know there was a difference. We just thought it was fun to crawl inside and sit like an Indian. We had to take turns and to us it was important to sit the way they did on TV westerns. We did projects in class: Indian headpieces with a band of brown construction paper and different colored paper shaped like feathers glued on, purple, orange, blue, etcetera. It never occurred to us at that age that real feathers didn't come in those colors, not in South Carolina at least.

A big project for South Carolina history was a poster board with a state map and pictures of products produced in our state around the center map. The really good part was making the map out of papier-mache. I remember we mixed flour with water and lots of strips of newspaper to make a thick white paste. I don't remember exactly how we did the shape of the state. There were no two states the same, so, everyone drew their own. I think each of us drew the state shape on thick cardboard, Miss Shumpert cut it out, then we each coated our map with the mixture, allowed it dry completely before gluing it in the center of the poster board. Then we painted the map green. Just imagine being in charge of thirty eight-year-olds spreading cardboard with that gooey mixture. Like I remember hearing from Uncle Leon, "There's not enough gold in Fort Knox" for anyone to agree to that. But that was the '50s, children respected their teacher and the rules. When our state project was finished, it would be debuted at open house in November.

***

The end of October we had the harvest festival. It was all about Halloween, ghosts and goblins, and raising money for the school. We didn't go trick-or-treating when I was growing up, kids living in cities maybe, but not country kids. We kids really looked forward to the Harvest Festival at school. Mrs. Shumpert helped with the fish pond. There was a curtain hung across the corner of the gym; two teachers stood behind it. You purchased tickets, probably when you got there, I don't remember all the details. To fish you were handed a pole with a line and hook on the end, threw it over the curtain and the teachers would put some little toy on the end and pull your line, then you could find out what you caught. We kids thought that was very entertaining.

You could also bob for apples in the big steel tub full of water with apples floating on top. Girls never wanted to do that because you had to put your head completely under the water to bite an apple, then it was yours. We girls were not about to duck under the water and mess up our hair.

Another highlight was the haunted house set up in Mrs. Robinson's room right outside of the gym. I never used my tickets for that. Kids would come out screaming and I was not going in. Mrs. Snelgrove's room was the bingo parlor; most of the adults hung out there. Goodies were on sale and the contest for Miss Pelion High and Miss Pelion Grammar was decided, which was based on money. One penny equaled one vote so the more money you were able to collect, the more votes you got. Sounds kinda like politics today, except the festival was for a good cause.

There was also the cakewalk around the gym. Music played and when it stopped the number was drawn and if you were standing on that number, you won a cake, all homemade and donated. Like I said, it was a fundraiser for the school.

***

After the Harvest Festival was Thanksgiving, making pilgrim hats and more Indian headpieces. Grandma always cooked a big turkey for Thanksgiving at home with all the trimmings, rice, giblet gravy, dressing and of course cranberry sauce. I believe we also had a Thanksgiving meal at school right before the actual holiday.

Christmas was the next holiday; the one we all looked forward to arriving come December. We had a party with cupcakes, candy, and other goodies. That year we, in third grade, drew names. I got a boy, Edwin's, name. Daddy went to town and bought a checkerboard and checkers for Edwin. I don't think he was impressed when he opened it, but he was a kid I remembered going to school barefoot, so he probably could have used socks instead of the game. Sherry got me two little plastic pins to decorate my collar. One was a poodle and one was a bear. Both were holding umbrellas. I still have them, residing in my jewelry box.

I never have thought of myself as a hoarder, but not everyone keeps the first tooth they had pulled by a dentist, a molar with long roots. If in the future I need to be cloned, I guess the tooth would be the very thing that could be used. I have been accused of keeping things way past what others would. I have all the letters I wrote to my husband and all those he wrote me. I keep thinking it would be lots of fun to get them out and read them to each other while polishing off a bottle of wine.

Back to Christmas at school, there was a Christmas program which the students participated in and some of the boys in my class were dressed as elves. They wore green felt outfits right down to green felt booties turned up on the end with a tiny bell. They probably didn't have a dress rehearsal or would have realized that skipping in felt shoes on the polished gym floor was not the best idea. The one thing I remember, all the elves skipped out on the gym floor and one of my classmates fell flat. Luckily, he got up and continued the routine. Actually, as it turned out, it was sort of the highlight of the program. It has been many years since I skipped anywhere.

In the classroom Mrs. Shumpert honored me with the task of drawing a brick fireplace with mantle and stockings hanging down on the blackboard. I used different colors of chalk, red for the bricks, brown for the mantle and so on. I honestly didn't consider it a work of art, but I was really proud of my efforts. Why she asked me, I'm not sure. I was however very pleased with the result. School was out for two weeks, but I was excited to get back to Mrs. Shumpert's class.

***

On Valentine's we each made a box for our valentines and the prettiest won an extra prize. Nancy won; hers was covered with crepe paper and lots of glitter. Daddy, of course, made mine out of a shoebox, covered with aluminum foil and valentine cards pasted on the lid. That was okay with me. Nancy's mother, Miss Laura Belle, baked cakes and she always made separate little heart-shaped cakes for her three girls to give to their best friends. Nancy brought three cakes that year and gave one to me. It was covered with a white sweet spread and the edges trimmed in red icing and candy hearts. I was so proud of my valentine cake. We didn't have themed valentines back then, no Disney characters or Marvel comics. My favorite that year was from Larry. He rode on our school bus. Nancy and I both had a crush on Larry and of course compared our cards received from him. I still remember mine. It was a large card with a cat in a fireman's uniform with red hearts, holding a water hose putting out a fire. The caption was, "I'm a cool cat, but my heart's on fire for you." I'm thinking it's a little weird that I can still remember that. I haven't seen Larry in well over forty years.

When Easter came, we, of course, had another party with cupcakes, jelly beans, large colored candy eggs with marshmallow centers, and chocolate bunnies. We had a big Easter Egg hunt for our class. Everyone brought three hard-boiled dyed eggs and Mrs. Shumpert arranged for someone, don't remember who, to hide them in the woods bordering the playground. There was a special gold prize egg and the child that found it got something really special, a live baby bunny in a cage. It was black and everybody really wanted that little rabbit. Two boys, Steve and Sidney, both found the lucky egg at the same time, so there was concern over who won the real live bunny. I don't know how that was decided, but as far as I can remember there was no kind of permission slip sent home about the prize; the parents were not asked whether they wanted their child to bring home a live rabbit to care for and clean up after. I hope they were as pleased as their child, because they were not consulted.

***

For Mother's Day, Mrs. Shumpert, requested the shop teacher have some of his students cut out sets of two large apples from thin plywood and a rectangle piece to attach to the wooden apples. Then each of the students in third grade varnished two apple shapes and the bottom piece, and glued the apples on each side. The finished product was a napkin holder for our mothers. I was the only kid in class that didn't have a mother at home, so I made the napkin holder for Grandma.

In the spring we had a fundraiser for our class. We were tasked with selling packets of vegetable seeds. We each received a green box with ten packets to take home and sell to family and friends. Each packet of seeds was ten cents and once we sold our initial box, we could get more boxes. Of course, the child who sold the most got some kind of prize. I, undoubtedly, wasn't the winner.

When school was finally over in late May, we would really miss our friends from school. We didn't see them for three months. We only had the one car that Daddy drove to work. He worked on the new house on weekends and didn't have time to take us to visit our friends. With no telephone, the only connection was mail. I still have a letter Sherry wrote to me in the summer with a cobalt blue stamp adorned with an image of the Statue of Liberty. It cost three cents to mail my return letter.

16. Vacation Bible School

Unless you were born and bred in the Southern Baptist Faith and lived in the country, you probably don't have a clue about the importance of Vacation Bible School. I will be more than happy to explain this phenomenon that continues to this day even though there is considerable change.

In the South I grew up in, Baptist Churches set aside a week Monday through Sunday in late June or July for VBS. All the kids from miles around had to be there. It was *the event* of the summer for country kids. It usually started late in the afternoon, around four o'clock and lasted for three or four hours. A lot of adults, men and women, participated so that we heathen kids could get a good dose of religion. Even kids that never attended church with their parents would come to VBS. It was first of all fun for the kids and non-attending parents basically got freedom from their little darlings for a few hours each day of that week, so they didn't mind letting their children participate. Surrounding churches also brought children to VBS at Steadman Baptist, and our church would support their VBS when their week rolled around.

We had to be scrubbed and dressed when Daddy arrived from

work, no bare feet, sandals were the normal footwear and for girls short socks with lace around the folded edge. Boys normally wore those black ankle-high basketball shoes. Daddy got us to church on time, the kids were already forming two lines outside to march into the church. Three children were chosen from all hands raised for the honor of carrying the American flag, the Christian flag, and the Holy Bible. Boys were chosen as flagbearers and a girl was awarded the task of carrying the Bible. Children were lined up according to their grade level and each had a teacher that marched in with them. The youngest class was Beginners, then Primary, Intermediate, and Juniors. Babies through teenagers attended. There was a nursery for the toddlers and babies provided so that young mothers who were teaching other classes knew their babies were being taken care of while they taught. Once we were lined up, the chosen three carrying flags and Bible marched in first. The pianist would play *Onward Christian Soldiers* or some similarly inspirational song for marching and all would enter the church. Classes sat together on the first three or four pews on both sides of the aisle.

There was a young woman who had volunteered to be Director for the week. She ascended to the pulpit and said, "Good afternoon children." The audience would respond in unison, "Good afternoon." The Director would then introduce herself and welcome all children and teachers. One of the teachers or the Director opened in prayer, praying for a safe and fun week for all the students.

It was then time for the Director to read the focus Bible verses for the week. There were usually two or three verses that were repeated every night and children were expected to memorize for our Commencement on Sunday Evening.

We then stood for the Pledge of Allegiance to the United States flag, the Christian flag, and to the Bible. First was the Pledge of Allegiance to the American flag, hand over hearts gazing on the flag held high by its bearer: attention, salute, pledge. We than sang *My Country, 'Tis of Thee*. I think the national anthem was considered too complicated for kids to sing, not sure. Next was the Christian flag, hand over heart, pledge, and then a song and finally recitation of the pledge to the Bible and appropriate song. Afterwards the VBS Director dismissed the children to their classrooms.

What lesson that was taught focused on the verses read at opening assembly. The Bible lesson taught depended on the age of the children. I believe the teachers received study books ordered from the Southern Baptist Association. Getting the children to sit down and listen was the biggest problem. There was always some craft that each class made. That was lots of fun, then we had refreshments, Kool Aid and cookies. Served outside, of course. Our liquid refreshment was mixed up in a huge steel tub, the same kind Grandma washed clothes in at home. In single file we lined up and one of the church ladies used a big aluminum dipper to fill our paper cups. We were allowed two cookies. We gulped down the Kool Aid, leaving a clown smile of color at the corners of our mouths, different colors depending on the flavor of Kool Aid. The older kids were more particular, but the beginner and primary classes didn't care about stain-lined lips and colored tongues. I was a member of the latter class. In-between drinks from the cups we crammed the cookies in our mouths. Then every kid started running and chasing each other or playing hide in seek in the cemetery, ducking behind the tombstones. The outside play was supposed to burn off some of our pent-up energy and calm us down. We had after all supposedly sat attentively through a Bible story designed to expand our Bible knowledge.

After our outside play, we were called back inside to be dismissed. We always sang a few of our favorite songs, *Deep and Wide*, *This little Light of Mine*, and *The Peace that Passes All Understanding*. All these included a lot of hand signals, foot stomping, and clapping. We laughed and acted silly with our little songs. It was like Revival for kids. Finally, the Director would dismiss with prayer and we were allowed to leave. Daddy was always waiting outside to pick us up.

Sunday night was our big Commencement ceremony. All the classes had something prepared to present to our parents and friends. Each class would line up in front of the pulpit and recite verses, sing songs, or present a little play. Then our teacher would present each child with a VBS certificate for attending and afterward we could take our crafts home. I still have my VBS certificate from 1958.

Maybe I do have some hoarding tendencies.

***

I think this would be a good place to talk about baptism and its importance to the Southern Baptist people.

One Sunday when I was eleven years old, I went forward during the invitational hymn we always sang at the end of service. I believe we sang *Just as I Am*. It was a big favorite for the invitation back then. There was no such thing as contemporary gospel and no instruments except for the piano and organ. Back then church doors were never locked and the community was welcome anytime to enter, sit, meditate about your sins, or pray. I went forward that Sunday morning, took the preacher's hand, and told him I wanted to be saved. That included being baptized. He had a prayer with me and asked for a vote of whether I could be excepted into the congregation. Of course no one would have dared to vote no. All hands were raised and church members came forward after the service, hugged me, and welcomed me as a new member.

Since I mentioned the invitational, *Just as I Am*, I am reminded of the time long ago, I think in 1956, when the Reverend Billy Graham held a rally at Fort Jackson in Columbia, South Carolina. Any time Pastor Graham had a televised crusade years later we watched every night on television. Daddy took us to Pastor Graham's rally. I was a small child and could not see the Rev. Graham for the large number of attendees standing between us and the speaker platform. I could however hear him speaking. When the sermon was over, we had problems finding our car, there were so many people. I don't remember Momma being with us or Grandma, who of course was not able to navigate such a crowd. We finally found our gray 1950 Ford. A man came up to the window and spoke to Daddy because he thought we had gotten into his car. Of course, that was cleared up soon enough, but that may have been the very thing that left the memory imprint in my brain. Since writing this memoir, it has become very evident that there always seems to be some insignificant little happening attached to every one of my long-forgotten memories.

Back to my baptism, about a month after my conversion, we had a baptismal service up the road from our house at the pond where we went swimming. Churches did not have fancy baptismal pools with warm water covered by a curtain behind the pulpit in those days. There were others besides myself who were to be baptized, girls, boys, and some adults. The girls were instructed to wear white dresses, the boys wore white shirts. At that time baptisms had to be held in the summer; didn't want no one to be ducked under freezing water. By necessity, sometimes new members had to wait for the baptizing part for months.

Pastor Abel waded out in the water; all those that had accepted the Lord waded out slowly forming a semi-circle on either side of the Pastor. It's not easy to wade waist deep with a dress on. He called each convert, one by one and we came forward. When he asked me if I wanted to accept Jesus Christ, saying yes, I was instructed, "Fold your hands across your chest, pinch your nose closed, and close your eyes. This will take only a second," he assured me. Putting his right hand on top of mine and his left behind my neck, "I baptize you in the name of the Father, Son, and Holy Spirit." I was ducked under the water, came up dripping and coughing, and was allowed to join the congregants on the bank, where I was immediately wrapped in a towel. I almost slipped getting out of the pond, but now I was officially in God's hands, backslider though I may be. I know I believe in prayer and have never regretted that decision.

Baptists believe it's necessary to make a public profession of your faith and that if you are truly saved, once saved, always saved. That Baptist belief has always been a comfort to me knowing that no matter, if I am truly saved, I have no worries beyond the grave. Everyone sins and no one is perfect. We were always taught that at church. It was before my time, but I have heard stories about sins church members committed; gambling, thieving, playing cards, or being unfaithful to their spouse. When these sins were reported the offender would be asked to come up and publicly confess before the congregation and ask for forgiveness. Of course, that happened long ago and besides you only need to confess your wrongs to God, not some body of backsliding Christians, gossips, and hypocrites. I have heard it said that you sometimes see the same people at the bar on Saturday night that you see in church on Sunday mornings. That doesn't mean you won't face a whole lot of trouble and heartache, we all do. I believe faith and prayer are important. I didn't mean to preach a sermon because the good Lord knows, I'm not qualified.

27. Rainy Day Fun

When we had real rainy weather and had to stay indoors, our imagination shifted into high gear. There was always something to do outside in clear weather, but when we were confined inside, we had to invent other entertainment. There wasn't a lot to watch on TV, especially since we only had three channels to choose from and daytime television was of no interest to little kids.

Often, we would make a fort by draping blankets over chairs or other furniture. The blankets became our roof, of course, we had to use heavy books or other objects to keep them in place, sometimes this occurred in the living room or our bedroom. Grandma's domain was the kitchen and we didn't want to aggravate her, especially if it was close to mealtime. We wanted to be able to play in our fort the whole day if it was raining outside. We would crawl into our fort, sometimes with a flashlight and of course our toys.

Sometimes we would play cards, Old Maid or Go Fish with a regular deck, but cards were so hard to keep up with, there were usually a few missing. I remember we did play Monopoly, we enjoyed that. The pieces that we moved around the board were metal. There was a dog, thimble, shoe, cannon, iron, wheel barrow, top hat, race car and Uncle Leon's favorite piece, the battleship. He would sometimes play with us, always insisting on the battleship token. We kids had our favorites, too. I always wanted the little dog or the thimble.

I remember bringing all of the kittens in the house and dressing them up in my doll clothes. That was fun and they did not protest too much. I often tucked them in my doll carriage, a long ago present from Santa, covered them with a dish towel or doll blanket, and wheeled them up and down the hall. They were all good natured but did protest with their sharp little claws when I would try to lay them on their backs in the carriage. They looked so cute walking around on all fours trying not to trip on the hem of their doll dress.

When it stopped raining, we would head outside, especially if the sun appeared. Any mud puddles we, at least Steve and me, were sure to splash through. Rainy weather in spring or summer, we were barefoot, and like all kids we loved to splash and jump in the puddles.

After a good rain we would play on the banks of our dirt road. The dirt was wet and more like the building sand Daddy had delivered to the new house location. The same sand that parents now buy for their kid's sandbox. We never had a sandbox; we had a whole yard if we wanted to dig in dirt. We would sit at the edge of the road and cover our foot in the damp sand pressing it down hard. Then very slowly we would slide our foot out. The result was a miniature cave we called a frog house. It was fun to wiggle our toes in the damp sand and build frog houses. Of course, as soon as the dirt dried, our frog houses would collapse.

We also would sometimes run under the car shed to seek shelter when it started to rain. The shed was a frame covered with tin and the rain falling on the tin made such a nice sound, we would sit on the dry powdery dirt or check out what items were on the braces of the frame. There was never a car parked under it. A wooden tool box hung on the back wall, rabbit boxes stacked, some lumber, the saw on the wheeled carriage, an anvil, oil cans, and lots of other objects we had no business having access too. There were of course axes, metal files, all sorts of saws for cutting wood, hammers, screwdrivers, and old tools that had belonged to Granddaddy Kelly. It could have been a dangerous place to play for nitwit kids that didn't have the good sense to stay away from these. We were country kids who knew what things were off limits.

I remember the story, told as a cautionary tale to us, about my Granddaddy Kelly. Granddaddy was splitting kindling at the woodpile one cold day. He would hold a piece up right and using a small hatchet split off small pieces. Well he ended up chopping his left index finger completely off. Back then there were no operations available to reattach the finger, just stop the blood flow with pressure and a heavy bandage. I expect he never used that method again.

There were little funnels in the black, dry dirt under the tin shed. We knew these funnels were where doodle bugs lived. A doodlebug was under the sand at the bottom of each. The funnel they constructed was a trap. The bug lay very still covered with dirt at the bottom. If an ant wandered into their funnel home, it would slide down the side and the doodle bug would come out and have a meal. As kids we would trick the doodle bugs. Taking a broom straw, we would gently run it around the funnel all the while repeating, "Doodle bug, doodle bug your house is on fire." Shortly we would see sand being flicked from the very bottom and a gray bug would show itself. These little funnels were also under the house where the sand was dry, black, and powdery. I know now their correct name is ant lions but we knew them as doodle bugs. We enjoyed fooling them. We even sometimes added a small ant, just to watch the trap sprung.

***

That old house still stands on Swamp Rabbit Road. The road is scraped every so often, mostly when one of the residents calls and complains. But if it rains for days, it is almost impassable.

When we rode the school bus, I never remember the bus not coming to pick us up because of the condition of the road. We had no house numbers, well to be honest when I lived there the road had no name.

The banks of the road were kept tidy by the chain gang. Think *O Brother, Where Art Thou*, the movie. The convicts wore black and white horizonal stripes, shirt and pants, they had chains around their ankles, and there was a guard with a double-barreled shotgun. I remember them cleaning the sides of the road, chopping down bushes. We kids stayed inside when the chain gang was working on the road; we thought they were dangerous. There wasn't a lot of trash to pick-up along the road. That was before fast food restaurants, so no cups or burger wrappers to toss out the window. Occasionally someone might toss out a beer can, but otherwise the sides of the roads were pretty tidy. People think nothing about throwing trash out the car window today.

We children helped keep the ditch and banks beside the road clean of drink bottles. We collected the bottles, put all we found in a big steel tub, and Daddy would take us to Mr. Cleve's store to collect two cents each on the bottles. That was the deposit amount added to the drink's price when they were originally purchased. Two cents each added up to a lot of change to spend on candy and goodies. Or sometimes, if we knew Daddy was going to buy us a drink, we would take an empty bottle as the deposit and save the two cents up front.

Once Steve found an unopened can of beer someone had mistakenly tossed it out. It did not have a pop top, so Steve thought using a hammer and nail would work just as well. Of course, whenever the top was punctured, the beer squirted all over brother Steve. I don't know if he thought he would taste it, but he got more of a taste than he bargained for. I think it was Pabst Blue Ribbon. Whatever brand, he regretted opening it, I'm sure.

28. Grandma's Daily Chores

Grandma never played any games with us. She was too busy with what she knew were her chores. I'm sure she was relieved when we all started to school and she had some free time, but she never sat down and propped her feet up in front of the television. She had no clue how to even turn it on. Back then, there were no remotes to operate the TV. If you wanted to change the channel or increase the volume, you had to actually get up and walk across the room and manually operate these features. If we still had to do that, there would probably be less obesity and no more "couch potatoes."

Grandma Florence was taught that a woman did everything required in the household. She never asked us to do chores. We were only expected to refill the water buckets and fill the wood boxes in the winter. She did everything else that needed to be done and never once complained. Her only relaxation, something that she enjoyed, was her flowers. How she got them to grow in our sandy yard I don't know, but she did.

She was always busy. When we came home from school in the afternoon, she would sometimes have a half cake waiting as a treat for us. She would mix up a cake batter without a recipe.

She would dump the ingredients in a bowl: sugar, flour, eggs, and flavoring, never measuring any part, then tilt the bowl and beat all the ingredients together with a fork. She would grease one cake pan, cut a round piece of wax paper for the bottom, then coat the pan and paper with flour. Knocking out the access flour in the trash can, she would pour in the batter and pop it in the oven. When the single layer was done and cooled, she would cut it in half, place one half on a plate, ice the top, then put the other half on and ice it, a half cake. Sometimes she would make icing with egg whites, sugar and flavoring, other times she invented her own. She made coffee icing with instant coffee or sometimes she just used jelly. She was a great cook. When Grandma made a cake and whipped up icing, if we were home, we always begged to lick the bowl. I know you're not supposed to do that with the uncooked batter, but never once did we get salmonella from raw eggs.

She washed and ironed all the clothes, which was a big job for any woman; especially before electric washers and permanent-press garments were available. Every piece of clothing had to be ironed, except underwear. Daddy bought her a new green and white ringer washer from Sears. It was such a big improvement from hand washing with a washboard in steel tubs. The new wringer washer was placed in the old smokehouse and drained out the shutter window in the back. Grandma thought it was the greatest. I had never thought there was electricity in the smokehouse because it was so dark inside, but I guess there had to be for the washer. When she ironed clothes, she sprinkled them with water and rolled them up tight. They were much easier to iron, dampened. This ironing was an all-day job, standing beside a wooden ironing board, hanging up shirts and dresses so they wouldn't be wrinkled or creased when we got ready to wear them.

She swept all the floors with a broom she had made with broom straw. She gathered a big bunch, cut down at the base. The straw was tied with heavy twine wrapped all the way round about a third of the way up the stalks, the remainder spread out with feathery wisps from each shaft of straw almost like wheat. These yellow-gold stalks secured tightly together with the twine made an adequate broom for sweeping up sand and trash.

Every so often, she cleaned the porches with a scouring mop. It had a long handle and a rectangle wooden piece attached. Holes were drilled in the rectangle part and scrubbing bristles were made from corn husks. All the inside rooms were mopped with a rag mop and wrung out in a bucket full of soapy water. The soap used was a bar of octagon lye soap, bought wrapped in red and white striped paper. It was considered an all-purpose soap produced by Colgate for washing clothes, floors, and bodies. However, I recall we used Camay soap for bathing ourselves, not octagon.

Grandma was taught her whole life how important it was to work hard and not to waste anything. When she received nice gifts of clothing, she wouldn't wear them, putting these things in her trunk, saving them and not using them.

I realize what a wonderful example she set for us. Except for the not using something because it's too nice. Why save things for a future we have no control over? If you like these things, use them.

29. Planting the Fields

One year in the spring Aunt Fannie and Uncle Willie plant- ed Uncle Leon's fields. I'm sure he did not require any rent of the fields. He would rather they be planted than remain fallow. Some years Uncle Leon let others, friends and family, plant his fields, but the big difference with Aunt Fannie and Uncle Willie planting the fields, they used a mule and plow, no tractor.

Their mule was named Cora and she did double duty for Fannie and Willie. She also brought them to the house in a wagon. They never had a car; their wagon was their only mode of transportation. They harnessed Cora to the farm wagon and it looked like what was referred to as a buckboard in TV westerns. The only seat was a bench seat with springs at either end. They always did things the old-fashion way. Riding in their mule-drawn wagon was a big treat for us.

Corn was always planted in the big field behind the tin carshed. That year Aunt Fannie and Uncle Willie planted the whole field in corn. I don't know what variety. I do know there is a distinction between corn planted to feed people and something called field corn, which people can eat, but was mostly planted to feed farm animals. Which variety was planted? I haven't a clue.

If corn is pulled when the tassels start to wither and shucked for people food in the South it is called "roastnir." Correctly pronounced it would be roasting ears. If the corn was pulled strictly to feed their mule and chickens, the corn ears would have been broken off in the fall, put in burlap sacks, and taken home to be shelled with a corn sheller, hand operated with a crank.

The cast iron gizmo was attached to a sturdy table with a clamp. The ears of corn were fed in the top by hand. A flat round disk inside had protruding metal spikes placed so that the corn would be pulled down and turned to strip the kernels all the way round. When the kernels were stripped the cobs and the kernels fell into a bucket. The operator of the hand crank also pushed the ears of corn into the top. It could be a dangerous job, one which required paying close attention. If you pushed the ear of corn too far, your hand could be pulled into the spikes.

That fall when the stalks and leaves turned brown, we all helped Aunt Fannie and Uncle Willie strip the dried leaves, bundle them together, and tie another dry leaf around each bundle. The dried bundles were called fodder. We went through the whole field wrapping bunches of fodder and sticking them on the then naked stalks. After all the fodder had been stripped and bundled, we kids helped stack them on their wagon for transport back to their barn to feed their mule, Cora. I don't remember them having other farm animals besides chickens but there was a large barn across the highway from the house they lived in with a mule lot attached.

They also planted sweet potatoes in the lower field on the north side that year. I have a memory of that because I was helping gather the potatoes. The mule was directed through the field pulling a turn plow to break up the dirt and expose the sweet potatoes. I was busy at my task of gathering the potatoes when I noticed a shadow above me. Looking up Cora was standing over me, just standing there. She could have easily stepped on me but she was really domesticated and meant me no harm. Of course, she did scare the devil out of me and I scrambled out of the way. The adults thought it was funny because they knew I was in no danger. I did not.

Aunt Fannie and Uncle Willie were two very dear people. Uncle Willie was my grandmother's brother. They had no children of their own and I'm sure they loved us. We surely loved them and loved to visit the house they lived in out on the highway. It was, of course, not owned by them, but it was very old and was considered a mansion when it was built by the Steedman family around 1790. It was a glorious place for us to play, in the yard and in the house. It was an amazing old mansion and a marvelous place for kids to play and explore, the big sandy yard and the old house itself.

30. A Historical Mansion

The house that our Aunt Fannie and Uncle Willie lived in was nothing short of a marvel to us kids. At the time they lived there in the '50s thru early '60s, it was known as the Glover Abel place. It was built long ago by the John Steedman family, quite possibly in the 1790s. It was considered a mansion in its day.

It was built so high off the ground on brick pillars. We kids could walk under without bowing our heads. We loved to play under the house. There were fireplaces built under the house where the Steedman Family had their slaves or servants cook meals. I don't know that for sure, but considering the age of the house and the fireplaces, I kinda doubt the family did their own cooking under the house. The house was so high off the ground, at least five feet, I would say. Under the house it was sandy soil like builders' sand, not black loam or dry dusty grey. It was like a huge sand box for kids. One section directly underneath the kitchen had three brick walls, open towards the back it was like their own tool shed, storage for chicken feed, and of course a place for their wagon and all the harnessing gear to hook up Cora to the wagon and the plow.

When we went for a visit, we parked beside the old house to the left. I remember there was a wood pile. They burned wood in the fireplaces on the main floor and in Aunt Fannie's wood cookstove. There was also a pitcher pump in the side yard where they could pump water for cooking and bathing. A little house or coop sat toward the back of the yard. The small building was for Aunt Fannie's little chickens, called bantams. She would let them out in the mornings to roam free in the yard. They would forage for insects and worms, but Aunt Fannie would also throw them a couple of handfuls of scratch feed. It was cracked corn bits purchased from the feed store or corn they shelled themselves. When the sun started to set, Aunt Fannie would call the bantams to their house and would prop a huge piece of iron, like a fire poker, under the latch to keep her babies safe from foxes.

There was also a large fenced area for her normal size chickens. There was a house for them to roost in surrounded by the chicken wire. I believe the whole area was also covered with chicken wire so they could not fly out. They did not roam free in the yard. She gathered eggs from these chickens where they had nests inside their coop. We kids were allowed to go in with her but didn't very often. We had too much chicken poop on our feet when we came out. We decided to observe the big chickens from outside their chicken yard.

The front of the house had a huge porch with what were fancy banisters at one time but had fallen in disrepair. I don't know who actually owned this magnificence house when they lived there, but it was very historic. I never thought to ask who owned it, but they may have let Aunt Fannie and Uncle Willie live there for free, just to keep the old house alive. The front steps, if you overlooked the devastated condition, could have been something out of *Gone with the Wind*. They were as wide as the red carpeted steps in Scarlett's fancy house in Atlanta. The only thing missing was the red carpet and the upkeep of course. The porch covered the whole front of the delipidated, archaic mansion. Besides the swing there were sad white rockers that had seen much better days. There were rain barrels on the ground at each corner of the porch. Aunt Fannie used that water for some purpose, whether it was for washing clothes or watering a garden, I don't remember, but I do remember them being there.

In the very middle of the huge porch were heavy, solid double doors that opened from this front porch into a huge hall, probably used in its early years for many fancy gatherings. I imagined fancy balls, with ladies in hoop skirts made with yards and yards of brocade and satin; gentlemen were dressed in top hats, cravats and waist coats. I know this seems like an exaggeration, but trust me, I pictured it every time I visited and entered that great hall. You would have to had witnessed this yourself to understand the enormous effect this beautiful and very old mansion could have on an impressionable young girl, especially one who was fond of fairytales and stories of the "Old South."

The only piece of furniture in the wide hall was a table against one wall covered with a beautiful crocheted table cloth. The table was almost unnoticeable in the width and breath of the hall. Of course, there were also double wood doors at the other end of the hall. These doors opened onto an L-shaped porch extending from the kitchen past two rooms pivoting to pass the huge hall and two other rooms.

With the doors open onto the porches or verandas of a bygone era, ladies and gentleman could step through the doors to take some air or a break from the Virginia Reel. Of course, this is just imagination, but highly probable in the earlier years of this historic home.

We never entered the house from the front porch, just played there. We entered from the side up a high staircase with one simple handrail. There must have been twenty or twenty-five steps up to the door that opened into the kitchen. In fact, it was kinda scary climbing the steps to the door, there was no landing. How Aunt Fannie and Uncle Willie managed for so long without a serious fall is a wonder. I think they brought wood and water in through this door. The steps were sturdy, but they were extremely steep and there was a screen door that opened outward, the wooden door swung to the inside. As a child, I thought the steps were dangerous and normally children don't even consider obstacles a danger.

***

The kitchen was a huge room, painted a dark gray. The walls were wide boards and the ceiling was sixteen feet high. With one wire dangling from the center of the room with a socket and light bulb for light, I couldn't even begin to see the ceiling. I do remember about half-way up the wall there was a hole about the size of a grapefruit and smaller holes peppered around it. I imagined it was some sort of gun shot, maybe black powder, but I never asked. That's one important thing, ask older folks. Uncle Willie or

Aunt Fannie may have known the answer. It was very noticeable. It was probably four feet above Aunt Fannie's refrigerator.

Entering the kitchen from the steep steps, to the left was her pie safe, the two doors at the top had screen netting exposing three shelves with dishes. Sometimes Aunt Fannie did have pies, cakes, or left-over biscuits in this safe. Air could circulate through the screen; baked goods were safe from flies, refrigeration would have caused them to dry out. At this time the only wrapping material for food would have been wax paper or maybe tin foil. I know that wax paper was used to wrap Daddy's lunch.

Around the room, past the pie safe was a window, then the green and white wood cookstove setting on four legs with a high back. A warming oven was at the top where cooked foods could be kept warm for a while. The stove was catty-cornered and away from the wall. This corner of wall space was the perfect place to hang pots and cast-iron skillets. The enameled green and white stove was always shiny, kept that way by Aunt Fannie. To the right and on the next wall were two windows, a cook table set between them. This table was where Aunt Fannie prepared her food, rolling out dough for pie crust, washing vegetables and mixing up dough for biscuits. It was also used to wash her dishes, using two dish pans, one with hot and cold water mixed and a bit of soap to wash the dishes. The other dishpan had clean, clear water for rinsing, then the dishes were turned down on dishtowels to dry. A flour barrel stood next to the cook table. Every homemaker of this period believed cornbread, biscuits, or hoecakes were a necessity at every meal.

Around the corner to the right of the cook table on the back wall was another window; past the large rectangle of uncovered panes was her refrigerator sitting to the left of the back-porch door. In the middle of the kitchen under the long cord with the socket and lightbulb was the kitchen table. It was always covered with a red checked, vinyl tablecloth.

The most important addition was the fireplace on the wall to the right. Above it was a mantel with a scalloped vinyl edging. It made the mantelpiece look nice and had a red and yellow pattern. Things on the mantel included Uncle Willie's spit can and his tobacco. Probably some what-nots, I don't remember, but I believe a picture or two. I think what-nots meant useless, breakable things for adornment, but really were just useless things that required more dusting. To the left of the fireplace was a pantry closet where canned goods and food staples were kept. I remember Aunt Fannie always had lots of Coca-Colas in that closet. She loved them.

The entrance to their bedroom was past the fireplace and in the corner of the kitchen. Just before you entered their bedroom was an enamel table that held six or eight water buckets, a wash pan, plus a dipper for drinking. I think they kept so many water buckets full because they climbed those steep steps every time they had to fill one.

In the wintertime there was always a blazing fire in the kitchen fireplace. Uncle Willie sat in his rocking chair to the left of the fire, wad of tobacco in his cheek, spit can on the floor, and stocking cap on his bald head. He loved to tell stories, especially ghost stories, and we loved to sit in front of the fire and listen to them. Of course, he claimed their house was haunted, and that I could easily believe considering the age and the different people who had resided there. Some of his stories included strange lights, balls of fire, and people in cemeteries.

If I was away from the fireplace, even on the other side of the room, it was very cold. Everyone had to stay close to the fire in winter.

If I walked across the kitchen and exited through the door beside the refrigerator I stepped onto the high L-shaped porch with fancy banisters covered with peeling white paint. Aunt Fannie had a flat thick board nailed to the top of the banister to the left that served as a place for potted plants. Then an opening between the rails for a set of steps, six or eight steps down to a landing platform, then another six or eight to the ground. These had to be added, not original. They would have been much fancier to match the banisters. These steps had no handrails of any kind.

31. A Night-Frightful and Freezing

I remember Grandma and I spent one night with Uncle Willie and Aunt Fannie. Grandma loved visiting her younger siblings and I frequently accompanied her. I did love my aunt and uncle, but as a small child I was not too keen about staying in a haunted mansion. No way would I have spent the night in a room alone. Grandma wasn't afraid of such nonsense.

I remember before bed we sat around the fire in the kitchen and talked, probably had a cup of coffee, but at that time, they had no television so we went to bed early. I remember Aunt Fannie removing the bobby pins from her ever-present, plaited bun on top of her head. Her hair was completely gray and it was very long. She always took it down at bedtime and gave it a good brushing. In the morning, soon after rising from her bed, she would brush it again, make a long plait and twist it into a bun on top of her head. Until the day she passed away, that was the only hairdo she had. Then she would head to the kitchen to make our breakfast.

Grandma and I slept in the next room to Fannie and Willie.

The door was closed. They tried to just heat the kitchen and their bedroom in the winter. The double bed sat in the corner on the wall next to their room. I, of course, insisted on the side next to the wall. We climbed into the bed piled high with quilts. It was freezing in that drafty old house, but I was well schooled for the situation because it was the same at home in the winter. We finally got a warm spot and I dozed off to sleep. It was pitch black in the room except for the little light that streamed in from the night sky. All I could think about was Uncle Willie's ghost stories, which he was so willing to share. I believe I only spent one night there with Grandma. I still loved to visit them but no more spending the night frightened and freezing.

***

The following day dawned clear and cold, but Aunt Fannie and Uncle Willie both were raised not to be idle while the sun shined. I'm sure the first thing I asked of Aunt Fannie was the same thing us children begged of her every time we visited during the daytime and that was, "Please Aunt Fannie take me upstairs."

She would say, "I will as soon as I finish doing what I'm doing. I have to get my chores done first."

Finally, she would relent and grab a big flashlight. There was a door that led into the great hall from the bedroom where Grandma and I spent the night. At the end of the hall towards the L-shaped porch there was a single wooden door. She would open the door and there were steps that turned two steps from the door and went straight up into complete blackness. Even in the middle of the day it was almost pitch black without a flashlight. I believe there were rails on either side at the top, not doors that had to be opened to enter. There were three rooms, each with a fireplace. The ceiling was much lower here and there was definitely no electricity. There was really no way to see how the rooms were separated, it was as though you could see all of them at once. Because of the dilapidated condition there was no telling. There may have been definite dividing walls at one time. Probably these rooms had not been occupied in decades, possibly not in seventy-five or a hundred years. I don't remember going upstairs at night; it was black as tar in the daytime with precious little light streaming in around the three windows, one at each end and one at the front over the big porch. These windows had been partially boarded up, if not it would have been lighter. I do remember thinking there would be no way I would spend the night in one of these upstairs rooms. After she had shined her flashlight in every direction, Aunt Fannie would ask, "Okay Catty, are you ready to go back down?"

I replied, "Yes, I've seen enough," and we began our descent back down from the dark. It was kind of a relief to see sunlight at the bottom as we neared the open door and reentered the great hall. Aunt Fannie always turned, closed the door, and latched it.

I do remember once when she took all of us kids upstairs, a bat flew out into the great hall, and had to be cornered and disposed of. I think we skipped the trip upstairs that day. I imagine there were numerous bats, spiders, and creepy crawly creatures in the three rooms, so it was probably a blessing we only had the flashlight.

32. Timeless Memories

When I quietly sit and explore the memories I have of the old Steedman home, I have so many thoughts about how we as kids perceived that old house and the huge yard. We absolutely thought it was the greatest place we ever visited. Thinking back on what I experienced, I am grateful to have had access to the old place, not just pass by on the highway.

I have described in detail the inside of the house through the eyes of a curious country kid. A few things I would like to add about the rooms in the old mansion. For one thing, each room was huge compared to standards of today. I would guess at least eighteen by eighteen feet, all were square, except for the bedroom we had slept in. That was because of the fact the stairs to the floor above made a curious-shaped protrusion from the wall to the left of the hall door.

There was another door leading from the bedroom Grandma and I slept in towards the front of the old mansion. This bedroom was closed off, but with an iron bed, made up with a chenille spread and side table. I believe all the rooms had a fireplace. That would make sense, because originally all the rooms would have to had a source of heat for the wintertime. This bedroom was never used while Aunt Fannie and Uncle Willie lived there, but Aunt Fannie had it decorated just the same. I don't remember what furniture was in this room, besides the bed. I only remember the side table against one wall, probably because of the curious decoration on top. Of course, every piece of furniture had to have a scarf covering, usually with embroidery or a crocheted edging. On this side table there was a scarf and what looked like a upside down bird trap made of small naked branches, layered like logs in a log home. It was square in shape and with each interwoven stick layer it became smaller until it peaked at the top. I think Aunt Fannie had added artificial flowers, roses, I think. I also can envision a full-length mirror with legs, probably also in this bedroom. The point being, with most of my memories, some small insignificant thing triggers the memory, like the odd bird trap decoration.

On the other side of the great hall there were two doors leading to what was, I presume, bedrooms in the early years. The one to the front had a bed and I remember the grown-ups saying Uncle Bunyan, Willie's brother, would sleep there when he came to visit. All I can remember being in this room was an old refrigerator, non-working of course, which had some items of men's clothing in it. I thought that was really strange, Uncle Bunyan's old socks stored in a refrigerator.

The other room held only a salt box. A rather fancy one, I thought. I went with Aunt Fannie to get some fatback from the box once. It was about two by four feet with a slanted top that had screen inserts. When we kneeled on the floor, Aunt Fannie and me, all I saw was salt. She dug down in the salt and pulled out the piece of meat she was searching for.

The old house, not taking into account the upstairs, was only six huge rooms and the great center hall. I can only imagine how beautiful it was when it was built.

***

The front yard of the house was surrounded by a rickety, picket fence, once painted white. It still had remnants of peeling paint. We kids loved to walk on the top board that held the fence together. If we fell off, we would simply get back on again. There was an opening in the middle of the fence at the front for the gate. There were Catawba trees on either side of the gate inside. We marveled at the large green leaves, more at the gossamer webs full of the Catawba worms. These worms were yellow and black with a horn on their rear, and lots of legs. Fishermen had long used them to bait their hooks.

We loved to run and play under the house and climb up and down the front steps. Aunt Fannie sometimes took us with her across the highway to the barn. I remember bales of hay inside and a trough where Aunt Fannie poured corn kernels for the mule Cora and later a mule named Martha.

Once Aunt Fannie walked with us beside the highway probably a hundred yards to a small cemetery under a cedar tree. There were some tombstones, broken and falling apart. This was the family cemetery of the Steedman family. I don't know if it can still be found, but I did visit there when I was a kid.

Whenever we visited every inch of the yard, even under the

house, had been raked by Aunt Fannie. I know when we left, she spent the following day raking the whole yard to remove our footprints. Her yards were clean and raked, her house was clean, neat as a pin. She didn't have much in the way of material things, but what she had, she kept in its place, clean and organized. The yards had few flowers; she wasn't much of a gardener. The only flowers were the ones she had in pots sitting on the thick board outside the kitchen door.

In the late sixties, Aunt Fannie and Uncle Willie moved into the old house where I grew up. Aunt Fannie was absolutely ecstatic, no more climbing the steep steps and she had an electric stove and a water spigot in the kitchen. Uncle Leon and Aunt Bessie lived elsewhere and we had moved by that time, so Uncle Leon asked Willie and Fannie if they would like to live in the old house. They left the Steedman house, leaving most of their furniture, wood cookstove, wagon, plows, and tools under the house.

What happened to the Steedman mansion? It mysteriously burned to the ground one night, either by people squatting in the house or by some despicable people that like to start fires. I was told it was the latter.

33. What is Death

When I was seven years old, I learned about death. Grand- ma Florence's brother, Uncle Bunyan, passed away. Before this event, I had never thought about death, at least not a family member's death. Of course, I knew that animals died. Uncle Leon and Daddy killed rabbits and squirrels for food, the big red hounds killed our kitten, and we sometimes found dead birds in the yard, but it was so dramatically different when we lost one of our family. Death was something I never in my young mind considered.

It was April of that year that Uncle Bunyan died. He visited us often, sitting on the porch in the evenings when the weather was nice with Uncles Leon, Eugene, and James and of course, Daddy. Uncle Bunyan would usually walk down to the house in the daytime to see Grandma, but in the evenings Eugene or James would drive him. His house and property were only about a mile from the old house. Uncle Bunyan lived in a wooden unpainted house just past the pond where we went swimming and I was baptized. The road crossed the pond dam, then there was a barn and the old house that both sat on a little rise on the left. The house, half the pond, and a fair amount of acreage belonged to him. Uncle Eugene and Aunt Ethel, and their family along with Uncle James, lived in the old house with Uncle Bunyan. I remember going there often before he passed away.

The day he died, I remember Tracy, Jr., came to tell Grandma. No one had phones then. Tracy Jr. was a young man and I think he lived in the big house that Aunt Corrie and Uncle Jule Smith once lived in across the pond from Uncle Bunyan's house. It was owned at that time by Robert Gunter, Tracy Jr.'s brother. Lu said she thought Aunt Fannie came to tell Grandma, but if so, someone would have had to bring her and that someone was Tracy Jr. The main reason I remember was because our dog Susie snuck up behind him and bit him on his heel. He was not the first person Susie had bitten. She also bit Aunt Fannie and Aunt Elsie, I know. Visitors had to keep a watchful eye on her. She didn't bark a lot. It was more like a lion stalking its prey.

The news of Uncle Bunyan's death just devastated Grandma Florence. She sat down in a rocking chair on the porch, bent her head down into her hand, and sobbed. I had never seen her cry before; it was very disturbing to me.

The hearse came and took Uncle Bunyan to be prepared for burial, and then he was brought back to his home. The gray steel casket was placed in front of the living room window. I guess he was the first dead person I ever saw. The casket was open; he had on a dark suit; a white netting trimmed in lace covered the open lid. Houses back then were of course not air-conditioned and the netting kept flies off the body. It seems almost morbid to even discuss, but as a curious child I noticed the little things. This was a new experience for me.

After they brought him home, we were all at the house. Of course, neighbors and friends had brought food for the family.

The funeral home placed a white flower beside the front door to signify a death. They also left a stand with a book for visitors to sign inside the front door and extra folding metal chairs for more seating.

I remember being there at night with lots of people in kitchen. It was a dining room-kitchen combined. Aunt Ethel's glass-front china cabinet sat up on legs in the dining area. It was dark outside. There was lots of food on the table, and grown-ups sitting around talking and drinking coffee. Then a very tall stranger walked in. I was impressed by the imposing figure. It was Uncle Bunyan's son, Odell. He had on a Navy uniform and a tan colored trench coat. The thing I noticed the most, maybe because I was sitting down and he towered above me, was his shiny black shoes. I thought I could actually see my reflection in them. The grown-ups all welcomed him and talked about him being in the Navy and from San Diego. When I realized he had come from the other side of the United States and that he had to fly, I was even more impressed.

There was no visitation at the funeral home in the '50s, at least not in the South. Folks were brought back home to be laid out in their Sunday best. Visitors would walk by the casket to view the dearly departed, usually commenting on how good they looked. Some people even took pictures of the person laying in the coffin. I have actually seen people do that. Why, I never understood. I do not want any pictures taken of anyone I love after their death. I thought that was just crazy. Why? At my young age I did not understand taking pictures. You think maybe they were going to frame the picture or put it in a photo album?

The one custom surrounding a southern funeral that I have

always admired, even in today's world with all the disrespect and flaws of others, in the South cars will pull to the side of the road and stop until a funeral procession passes. It is a timeless show of respect for the family and is still practiced, if traffic permits.

I don't remember Uncle Bunyan's funeral. It was at Oak Grove Baptist Church, but I have no other memory of the service or burial. I was probably with Uncle Leon because he always attended funerals, but normally did not go out to the cemetery. He would hang around outside talking with people he had not seen for years and I would hang around with him.

This was my first experience with death and it was decidedly unpleasant, especially witnessing my Grandma's heartbreak.

34. Traveling Man

If my Daddy had been rich, we would have traveled the world. When he was in school, geography was his favorite subject. He would have loved to travel and visit places he had only seen in books or read about. He gave me his geography book as a birthday gift years ago, printed 1927. Often when he came to visit, he would take it down from the shelf and leaf through the pages. He had underlined passages and written his name dozens of times on the page margins. Until he died, he could tell you the capital of every state in the union and he longed to visit them all.

We went on a vacation every summer, even after Momma left. Daddy, Grandma, us kids, and sometimes Uncle Leon and Aunt Bessie would go with us. Usually we would go to Cherokee, North Carolina, and drive through the Great Smoky Mountains National Park. The mountains were always Daddy's favorite vacation spot. This was before the interstate highway system was built. We would leave long before daylight and travel through little towns like Greenwood, Belton, Honea Path, Pickens, and Travelers Rest, heading for the North Carolina border and Cherokee. When it started to get daylight we were in the mountains and we kids would ooh and ah about the winding roads and especially going through mountain tunnels. Daddy would always blow the car horn in the tunnel and of course turn on the headlights.

We normally got a hotel room in Cherokee. The Princess Motel and Craig's Motor Court were the favorites. I don't know if Daddy made reservations before we left or we just showed up, as we had no phone to call. We rode through the Park, stopping at overlooks, taking lots of pictures. We always begged Daddy to let us wade in the creek that ran beside the main road, Little Pigeon River, I believe. New Found Gap and Clingmans Dome were necessary destinations. Sometimes we were fortunate enough to spot a black bear but had sense enough to stay in the car. We only spent maybe two nights because Daddy couldn't afford more, but the point was we had a vacation.

We would travel across the park to Gatlinburg. It was not a really busy place way back when and Pigeon Forge was nothing but a small community. Even after I was married, Jimmy and I stayed the night in Pigeon Forge for ten dollars. Back then ten dollars was a fair amount of money.

When Daddy took us as kids, he would always give us a few dollars to buy souvenirs. I still have some of mine. Big surprise, right. I've already discussed my hoarding tendencies but have decided that is not a problem with me; I just hoard memories. Anyone who has their closet color coded and has three hundred DVD's in alphabetic order can't be considered a hoarder. Right?

***

Even not counting Summer vacations, Daddy always wanted to go places and see things. The State Fair was always an important event in October of each year and he would take us. Back in the '50s during the era of segregation in the South, the State Fair was in Columbia for two weeks. The first week was for white folks and the second for black folks. As a child I knew no difference. My family was certainly not racist and never had been. It was just the times that we grew up in.

At the fair, there were lots of rides. Daddy liked the Ferris wheel and the roller coaster. We would ride them, and visit the exhibits and the building where all the farm animals were on display, their owners hoping for a blue ribbon. Once we children were given the most delicious glass of cold milk. I can still think about that glass of milk and how wonderful it was. I know it was organic. The word organic was probably not in the dictionary then. All animals were raised without pesticides in their feed or antibiotics and hormones ingested to enhance their size. Every crop and animal were raised organically, probably the reason my great, great grandparents lived to be ninety-five and ninety-eight even though they ate biscuits at every meal, lots of fried chicken, fatback and sausage, and everything was cooked with hog lard. It was all natural.

Let me continue with my fair story. I recall what everybody referred to as the "freak show," a man that was half goat; a fat lady with a beard; a human with horns on either side of his head; etc. There were always canvas pictures strung across the front and a man trying to entice everyone to come in and see these freaks of nature. We never did.

There was also what was called the "hoochy-koochy" show.

Scantily clad women would parade out on the platform, lots of glitter and feathers, and very little else. The "barker," I believe he was called, would try to entice the passing crowd to come in to see the peep show. Daddy would hurry us past this and on to the man defying gravity riding his motorcycle around inside a huge metal cylinder. I remember seeing this, he would rev-up the motorcycle and then ride around the inside walls of the huge metal barrel. It was somewhat amazing he could ride almost to the top sticking to the inside wall; more centrifugal force, like with the buckets of water we liked to spin around.

We really looked forward to the State Fair and would sometimes get cotton candy or a corndog, deep fried. I remember once I bought a hot pink fedora type hat with a long turquoise feather sticking in the side. My name was written in silver glitter across the brim. I wore it to school once. Other kids had similar ridiculous things acquired at the fair. Needless to say, that is one souvenir I no longer have.

Daddy was always taking us somewhere, frequently on day trips. We would go to Charleston to the Hampton Street Park, take a picnic lunch, and admire the swans and ducks in the small creek that ran through the park. There were flowers to admire and trails to follow and of course a zoo. It was not very big, but they had a bison in a large caged area with clumps of fur hanging on his body which was very dusty from rolling in the dry dirt, first one I ever saw. They had a cage with several monkeys; we loved to watch them. There were birds sitting on swinging limbs in their cage, preening their feathers and making strange noises.

After we left the park, Daddy would take us to the old Museum in Charleston. We loved to go there. I believe there was a sign inside the door to remind visitors to spit out their gum. The main attraction for me was the mummy, wrapped in gauze. I don't know who the mummy was, but it was ancient and the fingers peeking out were beginning to disintegrate, fascinating but spooky, especially when we knew it had been an actual living person.

After the park and museum, we would head home, but not on the interstate that was not built yet. Sometimes we would cross the two-lane Cooper River Bridge, one lane going and one lane coming. I was always scared to death to cross the bridge, but Daddy usually wanted to.

***

After Uncle Leon died, Daddy and I found a pack of negatives in his trunk. They were from 1957 and of course I had them developed. Some of the pictures were of a visit to the state house in Columbia, some taken on the steps and walking around the huge granite building. Momma was in these pictures. It must have been a Sunday day trip in the spring before she left. There are also some pictures taken from the car window of airplanes at the Columbia airport. We probably stopped beside the road to watch a plane take off. My Daddy loved to watch airplanes take off.

***

One night in October, 1954, checked it out on the internet, the Greatest Show on Earth was in Columbia, SC. The Ringling Brothers-Barnum and Bailey Circus still did shows under the Big Top, a huge tent where the center pole was raised by elephants. I don't remember anything about the clowns, tigers or trapeze artists, but I do remember this. When we were leaving the huge tent, we exited the wrong way. The elephants were directly behind us, each with a trainer. Grandma was concerned about the elephants and tripped over a tent stake. She was okay and the trainer stopped the elephant, but you can imagine how gigantic an elephant walking behind a three-year old would appear. That's why it stuck in my memory bank.

I always heard P.T. Barnum said, "There's a sucker born every minute and two to take him." That phrase was attributed to Mr. Barnum whether he actually said it or not, but it seems to be true.

***

One night in 1957, after Momma had left us, Daddy took Louise and Lula Mae to the movie theater in Batesburg to see a re-release of *Gone with the Wind*. Grandma had to stay home with Steve and me. We were in the living room where there was a fire burning in the fireplace and Grandma was ironing clothes. She had a big stack of dampened and rolled clothes to iron.

The living room set had only three main pieces: the sofa, a rocking chair, and a big side chair with massive arms. This set was an unusual maroon color. It was fabric with a fuzzy raised pattern but had been used so long the pattern was rubbed off in places. It was getting late at night – for heaven sakes that movie is about four hours long. Of course, we didn't know that at the time. Evidently neither did Grandma. Steve and I were laying on either end of the sofa and we were so tired.

"Please, Grandma can we go to bed, I am so tired," I whined.

She didn't say anything at first. I could tell she was not happy about the late hour and having to stay home with us and not go to the movie.

Finally, after I had whined and begged her to go to bed, she said, "You can just go to bed, it's right across the hall."

Well, there was no way I was going into that dark room and getting into bed by myself, so I just shut up and waited till they finally got home.

I didn't get to see *Gone with the Wind* until the 1967 re-release when Jimmy took me. I have the ticket stubs in our scrapbook. Surprise! It cost two dollars a ticket.

***

Daddy did love vacationing in the mountains, but on occasion we did go to the beach, Folly or Isle of Palms. We loved to jump the waves. We stayed at a beachfront motel and would get terribly sunburned. I have very fair skin and of course you don't realize how much sun you are soaking up until you take a bath and look in the mirror. There was Coppertone, but it did not have a lot of

UV protection when I was a child. After we got home, I would peel and shed skin like a sheepdog sheds his long fur.

Once we took a trip to Beaufort, South Carolina. A lady, Miss Lucille, Daddy found attractive had gone to the beach and Louise went along. Louise and the woman's daughter, Freddie, were good friends. We didn't stay at the beach but did visit with Miss Lucille's family while there. The house we rented had a very peculiar kitchen. It was a school bus, attached to the rear of the house. The floors were painted a blue-gray and it had the normal stove, sink, and dining table you would find in a kitchen. I don't remember the bus windows, whether they were all removed or just covered with curtains. It was really an amazing addition, one step up from the living area and you were in the school bus kitchen. All of us kids thought it was really neat.

Daddy kinda liked Miss Lucille and we would go visit her near Pelion, where we went to school. She had two children, Jimmy who was Steve's age and her daughter Freddie, Louise's friend. Freddie even came and spent the night with Louise at the old house. What do I remember about Freddie? She taught us how to make cinnamon toast in the oven. The strange things I can recall. Things didn't work out for my Daddy with Miss Lucille and she married another suitor, but we did love to visit her, Freddie, and Jimmy.

I think it says a lot about my Daddy that both Freddie and Jimmy attended his funeral over fifty-five years later even though he had no contact with them during all those years.

35. School & Bus Shenanigans

When I reached fourth grade, I got to move upstairs in the old grammar school building. It was like being an upper classman. My teacher in fourth grade was Mrs. Wolfe, wife of the local Lutheran Church pastor. She was a very kind teacher and I made great grades. I studied hard and began to really enjoy history.

Every week we received a *Weekly Reader*, which was basically a folded newspaper only front, middle, and back sections, the whole being the size of a piece of regular notebook paper. There were articles about what was going on in the world outside our little town, in places we could only read about, news from outside our little isolated southern bubble. We would read and study these articles in class. I remember reading about the transatlantic telephone cable. Per Wikipedia a phone cable called TAT-1 was laid by a ship in June 1960. That cable was surely the one we read about in our *Weekly Reader*. Communication by satellite was not yet possible. The space race was just getting fired up with the election of President Kennedy in November of that year.

One mischievous thing some of my classmates and I did was climb out the window of Mrs. Wolfe's classroom. The school office was a one-story addition to the two-story original school. I don't know when it was added, before my time. We climbed onto the flat roof of the office. I remember gravel covered the top and there was a short wall around the office. Of course, Mrs. Wolfe was unaware we did that. She was out of the room somewhere. Good thing we didn't fall off. That could have been a disaster.

I did really well in Mrs. Wolfe's class and in late August of 1961 I entered the fifth grade with Mrs. Hook as my teacher. She pretty much looked like all my other teachers, medium height, short curly gray hair, and glasses. Mrs. Hook seemed very intimidating and stern at first. She expected her students to do as they were told and follow the rules. As the year progressed, we didn't just stick to the textbooks. She was the kind of teacher that wanted to expand our horizons. We read articles from magazines like *Reader's Digest* and *Look*, studied poetry, and were made very aware of the Space Race and the Mercury astronauts.

In February 1962, we were privileged to hear first-hand the flight mission of Colonel John Glenn who orbited the earth three times. We were able to listen to the flight broadcast over the PA system. There was a big brown box high on the wall of every classroom so that the office could communicate with the teachers if necessary. On this PA system we were allowed to hear the entire blast-off narrated by newsman Walter Cronkite. We couldn't listen to the whole flight but every so often we received updates from Houston Space Center. It was definitely a historic event when his capsule Friendship 7 splashed down almost five hours later. The Friendship 7 capsule now resides in the Smithsonian's National Air and Space Museum in Washington, DC. I have been privileged to see it.

Mrs. Hook definitely did help expand our horizons and was a great teacher. When we came in hot, sweaty, and red-faced after recess, she would allow us to sit quietly and cool down. Usually she would read a chapter or two aloud of Laura Ingalls Wilder's wonderful stories. We always looked forward to coming back inside and listening to the next chapter.

***

Sixth grade found me in Mrs. Shull's class, still in the grammar school building. I had lots of friends and now the girls would hang out together in little groups discussing which boy was the cutest. We were beginning to leave childhood behind. We didn't play as many silly games. In October of that year I turned eleven-years-old, signed up for band, and joined the Girl Scouts. In band class, I played the clarinet, not very well, I admit. I decided on the clarinet because it was in small case that had to be lugged back and forth every day from school. I couldn't even begin to imagine carrying a baritone or French horn case home every day. I was supposed to be practicing regularly at home, which I did not. The cost of participating in band for the year was ten dollars, which included the rental of the instrument.

Our band director was John Helms. He was a cool teacher and when I learned enough from band practices at school, I joined the regular marching band. We played concerts at school and marched in lots of Christmas parades. We wore these old maroon and gold uniforms with a real necktie, gold colored. I never learned to tie that very well. The uniforms included a military-style hat. You can imagine maroon and gold did not make for a very stylish look. Before I quit band, Mr. Helms somehow convinced the school board we needed new uniforms and we got them. Of course, they were not the school colors, they were navy and silver, more stylish by far. How did Mr. Helms talk the school board into purchasing the uniforms and not in our school colors? He was always a smooth talker and the old ones were really ugly. The school board must have agreed.

***

In the South of my youth parents were fond of calling their children by a double name. There was usually a Billy Bob, Betty Lou, Lula Mae, Bobby Lee, Mary Lou, or some other double name in every class. All through grammar school I was known as Kathy Lynn. It wasn't until I got into high school that the Lynn part was dropped.

My sister, Lula Mae, changed to just plain Lu when she went to college. Daddy named her and where the Lula Mae came from, I have no idea. Louise was named Mary Louise by my Granddaddy. It was most certainly after his first wife, Mary, and his daughter, Louise. Grandma never seemed to mind at all. Names are not all that important, but I am glad Aunt Elsie named me.

***

I do have a few riding the school bus stories that are, to say, interesting. Our bus route, of course, traveled through a lot of sparsely settled dirt roads and with a high school senior the sole authority crazy things sometimes happened. Don't jump ahead of the story, they were all pretty reliable and kept everyone straight. There was no inappropriate sexual behavior or really foul language involved. We were all '50s kids and knew the appropriate bounds of a polite southern raising.

There was this one stretch of road where there were no houses, just fields of broom straw on either side and light poles. I don't remember who was driving the bus at the time, but I do recall two senior boys having a disagreement. I don't know what it was about. The bus driver stopped the bus and said, "O.K., you two get off the bus and settle it right now."

The two got off and had a fist fight in the field beside the road. It didn't last long but they both had cuts, bruises, skinned knuckles, and bloody noses. Then they shook hands and got back on the bus. It was settled.

Sometimes the older boys would get off the bus and race the school bus between light poles. The bus always won. I was not the only country kid with an imagination for entertainment.

Every afternoon when we passed Mr. Cleve's store out on the highway, someone would always suggest the bus driver stop and let us get off and buy a drink or chips. Sometimes the bus driver would actually stop, which I'm sure y'all can understand was very much against the rules. It happened quite often with our bus and if you had money you could jump off and spend it.

If the bus broke down or in one particular case got completely mired in the mud, the driver would have to call the school and they would send another bus to finish the route. Of course, seeing as there were no phones in private homes in the country, I guess the driver had to catch a ride to the highway and make a call. I know sometimes it took a long while for another replacement bus to arrive.

The time we were really stuck in the mud, all the girls went to the back of the bus, removed their shoes and hose, stuffed the hose in their purse, and carried their shoes when the other bus arrived. We had to walk through mud to board our replacement and the mud would have ruined our shoes.

After grammar school, all girls wore hose to school. Panty hose had not been invented yet. We wore garter belts or girdles with the hooks back and front to attach the thigh high stockings. I remember wearing a girdle when I weighed maybe ninety pounds. I definitely did not need it for support. Dresses or skirts and blouses were part of the dress code. It was not easy being a female back then. To say the least we were never comfortable.

Another bus story worth mentioning deals with southern kids and the issue of racism. I never had any black friends growing up, because there were no black families that lived close to us. That was the only reason. I do remember that our bus route stopped before crossing the pond dam where we swam in the summer. The white kids from Steadman attended Batesburg Schools.

At one point a black family moved into to the old house across the pond dam that had belonged to Uncle Bunyan. Going to public school themselves, the black kids had to be picked up by the black school bus. There was a white boy my sister Louise's age, Edmund. He was a real friendly guy and got along with everyone. Edmund went to school with us, but unfortunately had to move to Steadman, which meant he was in another school district. It didn't take Edmund long to rectify the situation. Since the black school bus had to pick up the kids at the pond, Edmund arranged with the black driver to pick him up at Steadman and carry him to their last stop to pick up the black kids. Every morning he rode the black bus down to the pond dam, the end of their route, walked across the pond dam to the end of our bus route, and our bus picked him up there. He wanted to continue going to Pelion. I'm sure this was not okayed by the school district, but no one was the wiser.

Pelion School was officially integrated my senior year. We had no problems and I made friends with the six new black students in my class. We all got along, contrary to belief, the South of my youth was not a hotbed of racism, at least not for us kids.

36. Moving Day

My daddy worked pretty much every weekend on our new house for four years. He had to hire someone to do the electrical work and the plumbing, everything else he did himself with some help from relatives. Finally, the day came when we could move in. It was March 6, 1962, and we kids along with Uncle Leon helped put things on Daddy's little wooden two-wheeled, one-axel trailer. It seemed like we made a hundred trips back and forth hauling all our belongings and unloading them.

It was cold that day and we actually had some snow flurries, but we were not going to be deterred. We were all very excited. We were finally going to have a real bathroom. The cabinets in the kitchen were not completed, only the skeleton was in place. Daddy still had to put all the doors on, the hardware, install the double sink, and hook up the water. Until then we had to use our washstand and fill water buckets, but there was a faucet right outside the back door. The back-porch cement floor had to be poured, for now it was just sand, cement blocks outlining where the porch would be and four blocks to step on from the back door.

We worked all day, kids and Grandma included, loading and

unloading furniture, clothes, bedding, books, and all the things that we had in the old house. Other people helped with the move, friends and family. Grandma was in charge of sorting all the things out as to what went in what room. There was a living room, kitchen, one bathroom, and four bedrooms. Louise and Lu had their own room, Steve had a small bedroom next to the bathroom, and I was assigned to sleep with Grandma. Of course, that was fine with me – it was all I had been used to for eleven, almost twelve, years.

We would no longer be heating with wood. Now we had a fuel oil heater that sat in the center of the house. This was the heating hall. There was a big silver tank behind the house sitting on a metal silver stand that cradled the tank. Somehow the oil was hooked up to the heater and fuel oil was delivered by truck. The heater had a blower on it and kept the house warm. Grandma's old rocker sat beside the oil heater. She sat there many nights and read her *Bible* and prayed.

We had started going to church at Pine Grove Baptist a couple years before we moved into the new house because the kids there went to our school. Steedman kids went to school in Batesburg. We begged Daddy to start going to Pine Grove. After all, our great grandparents, grandfather, and Aunt Louise were buried in the churchyard there. It was their home church. Daddy finally decided to leave Steedman church and move to Pine Grove.

Before we made the big move up the road, Daddy, accompanied by Uncle Leon, went to Batesburg and bought another vehicle. We now were the proud owners of a 1956 mint green Ford Fairlane. Uncle Leon almost certainly helped my Daddy buy that car. Uncle Leon was a very thrifty person, but he always helped Daddy with the cars because Daddy took him everywhere he didn't walk.

37. My Daddy Fell in Love

Shortly after we moved into the new house, Daddy became reacquainted with Jeanette Gunter. They had known each other all their lives, but Jeanette was much younger and growing up there was no romantic interest between the two. Jeanette was a widow who lived in a mobile home near Fairview crossroads. She also had four children, Willette, Donnie, Linda, and Steve. We of course knew her children from school. Willette was in Lula Mae's class, Donnie was in my class, and Linda was in the class with my brother Steve. Long story short, Daddy and Jeanette fell in love and we started visiting her, and she and her brood would come to visit us at the new house.

We took them on a day trip to Folly Beach. It made us feel like seasoned travelers because they had never seen the ocean. We have pictures of that day. Daddy, Jeanette, Grandma Florence, and "Little Steve'"sat in the front seat. The rest of us, seven children, were in the back seat of that '56 Ford. In those days, there was no seat belt requirement, no padded dash or air bags. We even took turns laying under the back window. We spent lots of time together that summer of '62. We kids would be playing outside our house, and Jeanette and Daddy would sit in the back seat of the car parked in the yard, holding hands and talking. I guess that was the nearest thing to privacy. This was in the daytime.

On August 11th of that year my daddy married Jeanette, so now she was Momma Jeanette and with two Steves, naturally a "Big Steve" and a "Little Steve" made perfect sense. Momma's Steve was only six years old, Daddy's Steve was nine. Everybody started calling them Little Steve and Big Steve, even at church and school.

Momma Jeanette and Daddy were married at the Reverend Richard Abel's home. The pastor's family was in attendance and all us kids were witnesses. Seven of us sat on their sofa; Louise was away at FHA camp. Grandma sat beside us, too.

Talk about mass confusion, we went through that for a while. Momma and Daddy went on a short honeymoon to the mountains and Grandma was in charge of all eight of us. Grandma was now seventy-five, so we were more or less in charge of ourselves. We got along well. I only remember one time there was a disagreement along family lines, us against them. That had something to do with our cat attacking their cat, I believe.

Life sure had made a big change since growing up in the old house.

38. Lessons Learned from the Old House

When I think back now, I'm glad I spent my childhood in that old house. Even though it was freezing cold in the winter and unbearably hot in the summer, I had a great upbringing. I didn't realize how poor and disadvantaged the rest of polite society might consider me and my siblings. We were raised to be responsible, independent, and had an imagination that knew no bounds and is lacking in today's youth. We could be highly entertained by spinning around until we fell to the ground dizzy drunk, leading each other around blindfolded, or simply chasing birds with a box of salt. Uncle Leon tricked us in that little episode. "You can catch one, if you can pour salt on its tail." That kept us busy for a whole day. We never for a minute considered what we would do if we did actually catch one.

Kids of our generation were taught to respect our elders, and how important it was to have faith in a higher power. None of us kids had a lot of material things, only getting gifts at Christmastime. Even back then, I realized that material things don't last. Being kind to every person, no matter who they are, or their lifestyle, is the important thing. I learned this by example from the adults who were in charge of my behavior. Daddy took us to Sunday School and church every Sunday. Meals were served with the whole family sitting around the kitchen table. The blessing always proceeded the meal. It was definitely a Norman Rockwell America at our house. Even though we might not have always liked what Grandma cooked, we ate it without complaint. Her fried beef liver was awful. I hated it. I would never have told my grandma though, fearful that it would hurt her feelings. Sundays were usually the one meal we all loved, fried chicken, rice, gravy, macaroni and cheese, always homemade biscuits. We never heard vindictive or mean things about neighbors or relatives. Not within our earshot.

Years later, I would work with people that thought it necessary to get all their children a gift when one had a birthday, didn't want any child to feel left out. But then no child could have their own special day. I definitely believe it can't be good for children to believe there are no winners or losers in this life, because there are. How will they ever face challenges and excel? Sometimes you don't win, that's a fact of life. If you don't win, lose gracefully. Strive to be superior at something and believe in yourself, that is the most important lesson. I believe every person has a God-given talent, we all need to actively seek it.

My generation was raised differently. We realized there were kids that were smarter and better at some things than us. Everyone has a special talent, everyone can surpass others in some way, maybe not in the same category. If children of my generation were determined, worked and applied themselves, they could achieve their goals.

When I grew up, I was not disadvantaged. I knew I was loved

and had adults I could depend on to steer me in the right direction. It was not an easy life, but we always had food on the table. I knew not to complain; I was thankful. We were always reminded that there were other children in worse conditions than us.

We never had to contend with an alcoholic parent that was mean, or a parent that would give us a whipping because they had to buy us a new pair of shoes. Every whipping I and my siblings received, we deserved. My sister may disagree. There was an altercation between her and Steve over her picture of "Kooky Burns" from *77 Sunset Strip*. I believe Steve snitched her picture, an argument ensued, and both were punished. She felt she was wrongfully accused in the disagreement. Except for this episode, my Daddy was pretty much, in my mind at least, "wise as Solomon" when it came to punishment.

Life was good for us kids in that old house. I grew up living on that sandy dirt road with no name. The road was in the sparely settled countryside away from city lights, sounds, and traffic. It helped me appreciate what I had. My childhood turned out to be one of God's greatest blessings. There's a lot to be said for quiet and solitude, nature sounds, a clear starry sky, no lights but the dark canopy above pinpointed with stars, and a golden yellow orb of the moon. Living at that time and place, I was taught to understand and treasure small things, a beautiful sunset, robins in the spring, and clear sweet water to quench thirst on a sticky hot summer day. Henry David Thoreau experienced such a life with nature. He once said, "What lies behind us and what lies ahead of us are tiny matters compared to what lies within us." What lies within me is a thankful spirit for that solitary life and an appreciation that I was fortunate enough to live it.

Epilogue

When I reread the three books I have published, I sometimes get teary eyed thinking of my family members; their lives filled with heartache and tragedy. Life is so fleeting and ends for us all someday. I was truly blessed and I miss those family members that have passed from this life into the next.

My Grandma Florence left us in November 1974 at age eighty-seven. She was a gentle, kind person who took care of my siblings and me during our childhood. Her patience seemed to know no bounds. We surely tried her patience many times.

Uncle Fred left us in 1974 also. He was a great conversationalist and never met a stranger. He suffered a fatal heart attack while fishing, one of his favorite pastimes. He did love to tease his brother-in-law, Leon, but they were close. Uncle Fred knew it was easy to rile Leon by disagreeing with him, all in good fun. They never, to my knowledge, were ever really angry at each other.

Uncle Leon went to sleep in the early hours of March 2, 2002, and woke up in heaven. When my daddy checked on him in the late evening of that day, he was gone. He body lay in his bed under covers, his glasses, hearing aid, and pistol lying on his chest of drawers, the way he left them the night before. I did love that man and it was because of that love, I started writing and recording the stories he told. I didn't want his memories to die with him.

Aunt Elsie died in May 2006. She had a completely different temperament from her brother, Leon. She was the perfect southern lady, quiet, reserved, and caring about the comfort of those around her. She loved Leon, even though he was not always easy to contend with, and my Daddy Robert. It didn't matter that Robert was a half-brother to Leon and Elsie, there was no distinction in their eyes.

My Daddy Robert passed away February 22, 2015. I still miss him and think of him most every day. He had Grandma Florence's temperament, a quiet, shy person, nothing like the stories told about Granddaddy Kelly and the fiery temper he possessed in his younger years. We kids could not have had a kinder man as our daddy.

Uncle Leon and my Daddy Robert lived to age ninety-one. Aunt Elsie was only three weeks shy of her ninety-first birthday. I'm thankful to have had their love and wisdom for my childhood and beyond.

I think about the despair my Granddaddy Kelly must have felt when he lost his beloved wife, Mary, then his daughter Louise at age thirteen. I believe that was why he turned to moonshine, but that couldn't cure the guilt and anguish he felt. Then he and Florence lost a son, Nathan, at age three. It seemed they had tragedy at every turn. It was a hard life for all of them, never knowing what tomorrow would hold. I'm thankful that I was able to capture their story, recording that spirit and faith that sustained them throughout their lives.

The Southern Child Lives On

I sat in the shady corner of the small balcony beside the sliding glass door to my bedroom. Behind me stood a wall about 'yay high'. In clear terms, between three and four feet. The white wall felt cool to the touch and bumpy. Before me a metal rail, did not hinder the view of this magnificent city, shimmering white in the mid-afternoon sunshine. All the buildings, almost monochromatic in sameness, stretched as far as my eyes could see. The horizon, miles away, ended in a range of low mountains. At least from this distance they appeared as a dark uneven line barely visible above the white structures. This is the ancient city of Athens, Greece, home to nearly four million people.

With my journal in my lap and pen poised, I began to describe through sight, sound and smell what I witnessed all around me. The apartment on the third floor gave me a great vantage point from my balcony perch. Dappled shade and sunlight fell across my journal as I begin to record my thoughts. The shadows falling across my lap and bare legs came from a large tree with slim, dark green leaves and a smooth bark. I was not familiar with this type of tree casting appreciative obscurity from blinding sunlight on my thoughts.

None of the buildings looked to be more than ten stories, all white stucco or block walls painted white. Some had red tile roofs. I assumed most in this section of the city, at least above the first floor, served as apartments. Single family residents are a rarity in a city this size. Describing what I witnessed with my own eyes, too amazing for words. A warm breeze blew gently against my cheek; the air had a sweet honey smell, perhaps some baklava being prepared by a Greek woman below or above me, near an open window. I was amazed that the city, so large with millions of inhabitants, was almost quiet. How I wished Jimmy was here to share the amazement with me. I heard a few dogs barking, pigeons cooing, the breeze touching nearby trees loaded with foliage adding a rustling sound in the May sunshine. There were children laughing and playing in the courtyard of the school below, but otherwise it was almost like I am sitting on my own front porch, except I was almost five thousand miles from home. Actually, it would be noisier on my front porch so near a busy highway.

I noticed the time; half pass two in the afternoon. I would later learn the solitude in such a huge city was a custom; the Greek people take a midday pause in the afternoons. All stores close for a few hours, only reopening in the late evening to continue their business. The only businesses open during this resting period were the coffee houses, which I soon learned was a major part of their culture. Greeks are more vibrant at night, night owls we call them back home. They are a people who love to socialize after the sun sets. This trait became evident when my companions, son

Jason and his wife, Anastasia, accompanied me to restaurants as late as eleven p.m. for a full meal.

The apartment where we now resided belonged to Anastasia's mother, Pavlina, a most gracious lady whose hospitality reminded me of my Southern people. Pavlina's apartment had beautiful marble floors, emerald green in the room used for entertaining guests. That room was filled with a sofa one could easily melt into, a few side chairs over stuffed with a soft, pale cream-colored smooth fabric, a pull-out table for guests to enjoy a meal and a daybed where Pavlina would sleep during our visit. Every room in the apartment including the kitchen, bedrooms and the living room had glass sliding doors and a small balcony outside. Only the bathroom had no balcony.

The most magnificent view was from the kitchen and the bedroom next to it. From these narrow balconies I could see the Parthenon sitting atop the Acropolis. At night it is lit as bright as a light house, only the lights are stable and seem much brighter, radiating from the base of all four sides of the Parthenon. It appeared as a shining jewel on a hill, its brightness beyond description. The first time I gazed on it, after darkness had settled on the ancient ruins, a gasp of astonishment escaped my lips. Imagine being able to look upon such ancient ruins from your kitchen or bedroom any time of day or night.

Before the darkness enfolded the city that first night, Jason, Anastasia and I took the metro to Grandma Mary's apartment and then drove back with her to Pavlina's. Grandma Mary, Pavlina's mother, spoke only Greek and was a gracious lady to me and complimented me on looking too young to be Jason's mother. At least that was the interpretation by Anastasia. Of course, I liked her right away. Being well past eighty years, she had lived in Athens all her life.

Riding with her in her car was quite the adventure. Her car sported a stick shift which she changed often due to the hilly back streets. I cringed in the back seat while she chattered on in Greek, and blew the horn frequently. Anastasia later told us she cursed at the pedestrians and other drivers that unfortunately crossed her path. To me it was more like the Space Mountain at Disney World. I just kept my eyes closed and hung on for dear life. That ride is one of my fondest memories of Athens. She was certainly a fearless and feisty lady. I couldn't help put feel that Grandma Mary and I were kindred spirits, living all our lives in the same place, sharing common traditions and the love of our families and surroundings. Though our spere of influence was thousands of miles apart, we felt the same attachment to our homes and the people we loved. Each of us were confortable with where we were in our lives.

We had other guests that night besides Mary. Two of Anastasia's cousins and their friends came for a late supper and lots of conversation, most of which I did not understand. One of the cousins did speak to me in English in an appreciated attempt to include me in the conversation.

We finally sought the comfort of sleep, after a traditional Greek meal which included quite spicy stuffed peppers brought by Grandma Mary, also a homemade crock of orange marmalade and of course Greek salad. The fearless Mary drove herself home; the other guests took the metro. I slept fitfully, so excited to be in this place. My mind was reeling from my first solo plane trip and the fact that tomorrow we would climb the Acropolis.

***

Breakfast the next morning was simple, coffee and cheese toast made by Anastasia; Pavlina had left for work at 6:30 A.M. At all other meals, I counted on Greek salad with lots of feta, cucumbers, and tomatoes. Of course, in a country where olive groves spread for miles on the hillsides and herds of goats' graze in the shade of trees, Greek salad is almost a necessity. These two things are mandatory for a real Greek salad, feta cheese and olives. I was surprised to learn an authentic Greek salad contains no lettuce.

After breakfast, Anastasia, Jason and I left Pavlina's apartment, taking the metro to the oldest section of the original city. Plaka lies at the base of the Acropolis where Pavlina was born. She is an original Athenian, a rarity, I understand, in this most ancient of world cities.

We bought our tickets and started to climb the wide, sloping stony path to the top of the Acropolis to the Parthenon. The stones in the path were worn smooth from so many feet that had trodden this same path over the centuries. The stones, some large, required walking slowly and gingerly on the rocky path. Anyone could easily trip. Watching my footsteps gave me cause to examine the smooth worn stones more closely. They were gray, pink, white, even black, different colors but all leading upward. Thousands, probably millions of ancient people had trod this path. The Parthenon had almost a spiritual component. Once white, the towering Doric columns were honey colored, after centuries of pollution and disuse. It was humbling to gaze on the ancient structure, aware that these marble columns were carved over two thousand years ago.

***

We left Athens the next day traveling to the city of Tripoli on the Peloponnesian peninsula. Anastasia drove, because unless you live there permanently, the streets are much like a NASCAR race without the continuous left turn. There didn't seem to be well-marked lanes, everyone traveled fast, the side rear view mirrors folded in and motorcycles were whipping in and out between the cars. The only traffic rule on the main thoroughfare seemed to be everyone traveling in the same direction. It took two hours to get out of this sprawling metropolis and in to the sparsely settled country side. No amount of money would entice me to drive in Athens, Greece. Atlanta is a walk in the park compared to Athens. Managing a motor vehicle through this ancient city was a talent one seems to have been born with, like Grandma Mary. It's no wonder Greece has the highest auto fatality rate in Western Europe.

After a week-long visit with Anastasia's father, and brother, we three travelers borrowed one of Homer's cars, traveled to Kalamata where we bought ferry tickets for the island of Crete. The ferry boat was a behemoth of a vessel that left Kalamata in the late afternoon. We drove our car onto the ferry along with many others, including huge trucks carrying cargo containers. Below, the main deck was packed with all manner of vehicles. Our trip to the island of Crete would take seven to eight hours crossing the Mediterranean Sea.

Standing on the deck with the sun hanging low on the horizon, I couldn't help but recall my uncle's war stories of these beautiful blue-black waters he had crossed so many years before.

What he had said was true; the Mediterranean was so blue it appeared almost purple, the white capped waves created such a contrast. I was having so many memorable firsts on this trip across the Atlantic: flying solo, seeing the ancient city of Athens and, most of all, the privilege of staying with Greek people instead of a tour group. How fortunate I considered myself at that moment.

I was born in the Deep South, spent my childhood not a mile from the North Edisto River in South Carolina. I grew up in the same old house built by my grandfather. No indoor plumbing, burning wood to ward off the fierce cold in the winter, no air conditioning or even electric fans to cool the humid summer days and nights of July and August. The road we lived on was mostly sand beds. They could quickly mire a car in the loose soil, like quick sand without the water. There was nothing that hinted I would one day travel across oceans, see orchards of olive and lemon trees and actually visit cities mentioned in the Bible. My father worked in a cotton mill, my mother in a sewing room. We were poor but never suffered for the lack of money. We had the necessities, food, shelter, clothing and unlimited forest, fields and swamps to explore. I was connected to the land and had lots of friends and relatives. I am a Southern Child.

Photographs

Momma Sallie

Lula Mae & Louise

Aunt Elsie Ridgell, my Daddy's sister,
holding Kathy, the author

Louise, me in tub & Lula Mae

Louise, Kathy & Lula Mae, I was just learning to walk with a little help from Lu

KATHY G. WIDENER

Louise, Lula Mae & Kathy 1952
This was Lula Mae's 4th birthday, I was 20 months old

Kathy 1952, would love to have that wagon now

Kathy 1st birthday Oct. 1952

Kathy's 1st Birthday

Lula Mae holding Steve 1953

THE SOUTHERN CHILD

Steve 1954

All of us in front of 1950 Ford

Aunt Bessie 1957

Grandma at the spigot 1957

Leon 1957

Momma Sallie

Elsie, Fred and Grandma with her apron on

Me & Steve with Susie's puppies 1957

THE SOUTHERN CHILD

Me standing beside the walnut tree

Steve with puppy, Momma & Louise 1957

THE SOUTHERN CHILD

MAY 1957

Kids in front yard

Louise and Lula Mae playing school

THE SOUTHERN CHILD

Girls at the walnut tree

Kathy 2nd grade

Girls at the State House

Daddy & Steve at the State Fair in Columbia, SC

Kids at Hampton Park, Charleston

Outhouse

House at Rayflin

Uncle Olin, Aunt Jennie & Rascal, their pet raccoon

Virginia, Aunt Jennie and Mildred, the way I remember them

THE SOUTHERN CHILD

Mountain Vacation

Kids & Elsie, sister of our Daddy Robert

THE SOUTHERN CHILD

Christmas at the old house

Uncle Bunyan, Grandma Florence's
brother & friend

Odell Burkett, Uncle Bunyan's son

Me in my dress made from flour sacks, standing beside Grandma's rose bush

Vacation Bible School at Steadman Baptist Church 1958 or 59
(author 6th child from right in front row)

The Steadman House. Aunt Fannie and Uncle Willie, Grandma brother, lived in this house. We loved to visit there

Steadman House 1971

Charleston trip in 1962. Daddy & Jeanette (soon to be his wife) with her children, grandma and us. The only one missing is Willette, she must have taken the photo

www.ingramcontent.com/pod-product-compliance
Lightning Source LLC
Chambersburg PA
CBHW030107100526
44591CB00009B/318